HAC

Vins
de Pays

A Buyer's Guide
to the Best
French Country Wines

Foreword by Tim Atkin

MITCHELL BEAZLEY

Vins de Pays

A Buyer's Guide to the Best French Country Wines

This edition published in 2004 by Mitchell Beazley, an imprint of Octopus Publishing Group Ltd, 2–4 Heron Quays, London E14 4JP

Originally sourced from *The Hachette Guide to French Wines 2004*.
Editorial director: Catherine Montalbetti

The editorial director wishes to thank the *Office National Interprofessionnel des Vins*, ONIVINS, and its regional delegations, for their contribution.

A CIP catalogue record for this book is available from the British Library.

ISBN 1 84000 953 5

For the English Translation:
Managing editor
Hilary Lumsden

Art direction
Yasia Leedham-Williams
Tim Pattinson

Typeset in Aldus and Shannon

Printed and bound by Mackays Ltd in the UK

CONTENTS

4 Foreword

11 The Loire Valley

30 Aquitaine and Charentes

43 The Garonne

54 Languedoc-Roussillon

102 Provence, the Lower Rhône Valley, and Corsica

126 The Alps and the Southeast

135 The Northeast

142 Index

KEY

Red wine

White wine

Rosé wine

Aged in cask

Aged in vat

Temperature regulated

For sale on the premises

Good value for money

€ Average bottle price in France (in euros) per case of twelve

🏆 Tasting panel's special selection

☆ Good wine

☆☆ Excellent wine

☆☆☆ Exceptional wine

Foreword

It's no comment on the quality of the wine concerned, but a *vin de pays* red was the catalyst for one of the biggest arguments I've ever had with a sommelier. It occurred in a restaurant with a celebrated wine list. Drinking to a budget, a friend and I kicked off with a decent white Bordeaux, then moved on to a blended Vin de Pays d'Oc, with the main course.

Or rather we didn't. I thought the wine was corked and sent it back. The wine waiter disagreed. "You don't understand the style," he told me, "it's supposed to taste like that." I knew the wine well and told him he was talking drivel. Straightening his black apron, he curled his lip and looked me in the eye. "Since you have ordered a *petit vin*, monsieur, (the insult sounds better in French than it would have done in English), I will replace it with something else. Otherwise…"

The insult sailed several feet over my head. For a start, in my opinion, no-one but a snob would describe the particular wine we were drinking as a *"petit vin"*. (I've still got bottles from the early 1990s in my cellar and they are drinking beautifully at the moment. I showed one to a Californian winemaker friend only the other night and he thought it was a top Gigondas or Châteaneuf-du-Pape.) Secondly, what's wrong with drinking a "little wine" anyway? Not even Sir Andrew Lloyd Webber lives by *grand cru* Burgundy and First Growth claret alone; even if I could afford to drink fine wines with every meal, I wouldn't. And thirdly, the idea that *vins de pays* are necessarily inferior to appellation wines should have been ushered towards the nearest spittoon some time ago. There are good, average, and poor appellation wines, often bearing some very swanky names, just as there are good, average, and poor *vins de pays*.

My own interest in *vins de pays*, specifically the wines of the Vins de Pays d'Oc, which account for over a third of France's country wine production, dates back to the early 1990s. Someone asked me to write a book about the winemaking revolution that was taking place in the Languedoc-Roussillon, an area that was casting off its image as a producer of the sort of stuff served from a jerry can, to embrace new marketing and winemaking ideas. It took me about half a second to agree to accept the commission, and not just because I love the smells, the warmth, and the flavours of the Mediterranean.

I wanted to see how France planned to confront the threat posed by the New World. How would it cope, intellectually and oenologically, with the idea of producing modern, consumer-focused varietal wines, where the name of the variety was as important as its origin, wines with fruit and easy-drinking appeal?

The Languedoc-Roussillon (or the Midi as it is known in France) is not the only part of France that produces *vins de pays*, but with more than seventy per cent of the total country wine volume (7.4 million hectolitres out of an annual production of around ten million hectolitres, with Vin de Pays d'Oc, Vin de Pays de l'Hérault, and Vin de Pays de l'Aude all important names in their own right), it is the most important. So what I discovered there represented a large part of the overall *vin de pays* picture.

And what did that picture look like ten years ago? Well, the Australian imprint was real, either from companies like BRL Hardy, who had set up a cellar (Domaine de la Baume) in the region, or from individuals (James Herrick, Hugh Ryman) who had worked Down Under and been heavily influenced by the Aussie way of doing things. But it wasn't just a case of the Riverland transported to the south of France. There were plenty of French innovators and visionaries, from Robert Skalli of Fortant de France, Olivier Mandeville of Domaine Mandville, and Aimé Guibert of Mas de Daumas Gassac to cooperatives like Foncalieu and Val d'Orbieu.

I was also surprised by the diversity of the region's *vins de pays*, even then. There were plenty of varietal Chardonnays, Sauvignon Blancs, Syrahs, and Merlots (though not as many as there are now) and a couple of very good Viogniers and Pinot Noirs, but there were also some very good blended wines. Some of these *vins de pays*, inspired by the Médoc style, acquired great notoriety, as you will find in this book.

In the intervening decade, a number of top Languedoc-Roussillon producers have taken the decision to bottle some or all of their wines as *vins de pays*. The majority also make wines under the appellation system, but use the looser *vin de pays* rules to fashion certain, arguably more experimental wines. They might produce white wines whose high alcohol levels would disqualify them from appellation status; they might wish to make a varietal Syrah in an AC area that demands a blend of grape varieties.

In this sense (and this is not to be underestimated in a country whose regulations can stifle innovation as well as preserving the best aspects of traditionalism) *vins de pays* are an important outlet for maverick spirits. Aimé Guibert of Mas de Daumas Gassac and Eloi Durbach of Domaine de Trévallon in Provence (who sells his brilliant Cabernet/Syrah blend as a humble-sounding Vin de Pays des Bouches du Rhône) are the most famous examples.

Traditionalists often criticize *vins de pays* as simple, fruity wines that have little or no heritage and could come from almost anywhere, but they are wrong on several counts.

Let's deal with the heritage bit first. The term *vin de pays* has been in use since the 1930s, although it wasn't formalized until September 1979, and is legally defined as a table wine carrying the geographical indication of the sector, region or département from where it originates. At that time the first guidelines were established for production methods, yields, and recommended grape varieties. This directive was updated in September 2000, when the regulations were extended to cover things like alcohol content, acidity levels, and permitted additives. Local committees also impose their own rules on their members, although these are nothing like as constrictive as those faced by appellation producers, particularly where grape varieties are concerned.

It is also untrue that *vins de pays* have no sense of place or origin. There are three categories of *vins de pays*, each of which is tied to a specific region or geographical area. Alright, some of the regions can be pretty large, but the wines still have a recognizable home. The first category is made up of wines from a designated area (Vin de Pays de St Guilhem Le Désert, Vin de Pays des Coteaux de Murviel or Vin de Pays de la Côte Vermeille, for example). Some of these are almost unknown, even to the people who live there, but, numerically at least, they make up the majority of France's 140-odd *vins de pays*. The second category is made up of wines named after their department of origin (Vaucluse, Hérault, Pyrénées Orientales, etc), while the third category is, geographically speaking, the loosest of all, consisting of five, large regional zones. These are Jardin de la France (in the Loire), Comté Tolosan (Midi-Pyrénées), Pays d'Oc (Languedoc-Roussillon), Comtés Rhodaniens (Rhône-Alpes) and the recently extended Portes de la Mediterranée (Corsica, the Drôme, the Ardèche, and Provence). These three categories together are responsible for twenty-seven per cent, thirty-four per cent and thirty-nine per cent of *vin de pays* production, respectively.

The majority of *vins de pays* are what the French call "*vins de cépages*" and the English-speaking world calls varietal wines – that is wines that are labelled according to grape variety. In fact, with a few exceptions in Alsace and the Loire Valley, they are the only way a consumer can buy a French wine labelled with the name of a grape, be it Chardonnay, Merlot, Terret or Marselan. To a considerable extent, *vins de pays* are a response to the marketing and winemaking initiatives of the New World, where producers have simplified wine styles to appeal to a broader cross-section of consumers. Names such as Vin de Pays d'Oc (3.5 million hectolitres) or Vin de Pays de l'Aude (1.2 million hectolitres) have almost become brands in their own right, offering styles that can compete with entry level wines from the southern hemisphere.

At a time when French viticulture struggles to sell wines at profitable prices without government and/or EU intervention), the *vin de pays* category is doing very well. Between 1980 and 2000, *vin de pays* production rose from four million hectolitres to its current level of around ten million hectolitres.

It's also worth remembering that the success of certain *vins de pays*, especially in the UK, Germany, and the USA, has had important socio-economic consequences. Agriculture in the region of Gascony, for example, where the wines were traditionally distilled to make armagnac, has been remodelled thanks to the emergence of Vin de Pays des Côtes de Gascogne. Commercial successes of this *vin de pays* have shown that a region renowned for its eau-de-vie can also make a name for itself with wines made from local or international grapes. In the process, they have kept a lot of grape growers in business.

The same is true of the Languedoc-Roussillon, where *vins de pays* have been embraced by the cooperative movement as a way of shifting large quantities of wine. It doesn't always pay to make *vins de pays*, but one recent statistic is particularly telling: in the first ten months of 2002, *vins de pays* from the Midi increased by ten per cent in volume and value on export markets.

And what about the charge that *vins de pays* are simple wines designed to appeal to the masses? There is certainly some truth to this, although fruit and simplicity are not necessarily a crime against vinous French culture. When they were created, *vins de pays* were intended to represent a bridge between basic *vin de table* and appellation wines. It is a function that, more often than not, they still fulfil with cheery good humour.

There are some very complex wines produced under *vins de pays* labels, but most of the time, these are wines that are as easy to understand as they are to drink. Most of them come from the south of France (eighty-five per cent according to the latest figures) and the wines reflect the warmth and easy-going lifestyle of the region. But wherever they come from, *vins de pays* are usually meant for quaffing rather than contemplation. That's what this book is all about. So grab yourself a corkscrew, assemble a few friends around a table and get drinking.

Tim Atkin MW

The Loire Valley

The wines of the Jardin de la France, a regional classification, currently make up ninty-five per cent of *vin de pays* production in the Loire Valley, a vast territory comprising no fewer than thirteen *départements*: Maine-et-Loire, Indre-et-Loire, Loiret, Loire-Atlantique, Loir-et-Cher, Indre, Allier, Deux-Sèvres, Sarthe, Vendée, Vienne, Cher, and Nièvre. Additionally, the classification includes *vins de pays* from *départements* and other localities such as the *vins de pays* of Retz (south of the Loire estuary), the Marches de Bretagne (southeast of Nantes), and the Coteaux Charitois (around Charité-sur-Loire).

Total production in the region is currently running at some 617,000 hl, for the greatest part comprising traditional Loire grape varieties. Whites represent around forty-five per cent and are typically dry, fresh, and fruity, made from Chardonnay, Sauvignon Blanc, and Grolleau Gris grapes. Reds and rosés are made from Gamay, Cabernet, and Grolleau Noir grape varieties. Generally speaking, these *vins de pays* should be drunk young, although the occasional Cabernet vintage may benefit from cellaring.

CHER

VENESMES
Sauvignon 2002

2.2 hectares   6,000 bottles

**SCEV de Venesmes, 18190 Venesmes
tel. 06.08.23.59.04, fax 02.48.60.68.01
Tasting: by appt.**

 € 3-5

COTEAUX CHARITOIS

DOMAINE DU PUITS DE COMPOSTELLE
Pinot Noir Elevé en Fût de Chêne 2002☆

1 hectare   3,000 bottles

This estate opened for business in 1999 on the initiative of a number of oenologist friends who acquired a small vineyard on the pilgrim's route to Santiago de Compostela. The still-young Pinot Noir grape variety yields a typical blackberry nose and taste accompanied by distinct tannins, which will develop over time to produce a balanced wine.

**Dom. du Puits de Compostelle, 11, bis Cours du Château,
58400 La Charité-sur-Loire,
tel. 03.86.70.03.29, fax 03.86.70.06.74,
e-mail puitsdecompostelle@st.fr
Tasting: by appt.**

 € 5-8

DOMAINE DE LA VERNIERE
Pinot Noir 2002☆
1.4 hectares   8,500 bottles

Denis Beaulieu cultivates this six-hectare vineyard surrounding an eighteenth and ninteenth century château. The Pinot Noir grape used has resulted in a manifestly young wine – its aromas have yet to emerge fully but augur well. This is a structured wine that should reveal its full potential a few years from now. The harmonious Chardonnay 2002 was also noted.

Dom. de la Vernière, La Vernière, 58350 Chasnay,
tel. 03.86.70.06.74, fax 03.86.70.06.74
Tasting: by appt. Prop: Simon Beaulieu

    € 5-8

JARDIN DE LA FRANCE

ADEA CONSULES
Ligéria 2000☆☆
0.8 hectares   3,000 bottles

Cabernet Franc, Cabernet Sauvignon, Merlot, and Cot varieties are blended and stored in cask for nineteen months to yield this dark and intense wine with an expressive nose of wood notes and pleasant spices. The wine is rich on the palate, with the merest hint of cask, that will soon give way to other aromas.

Adéâ Consulès, 3, rue Saint-Martin, 49540 Martigné-Briand,
tel. 02.41.59.19.51, fax 02.41.59.16.86,
e-mail bpaumard@ansf.net
Tasting: by appt. Prop: B. Paumard

   € 30-38

DOMAINE DES CHEVRIERES
Gamay 2002☆☆
5 hectares   18,000 bottles

Martine and Christophe Réthoré's richly coloured wine has luminous highlights and ripe-fruit aromas. Well-balanced and rich it will age. Cabernet 2002 and Pinot Noir 2002 also good.

**Vignoble Réthoré, Les Vignes, 49110 Saint-Rémy-en-Mauges,
tel. 02.41.30.12.58, fax 02.41.46.35.44
Tasting: by appt.**

DOMAINE DE LA COCHE
Cabernet 2002☆
2 hectares   6,000 bottles

In 1991, two young winemakers set up this twenty-one-hectare estate planted with eight grape varieties. This purple wine has blackcurrant aromas and is well-structured. It is fresh, round, and balanced, and will go well with roast beef.

**Emmanuel Guitteny, Dom. de la Coche, 44680 Sainte-Pazanne,
tel. 02.40.02.44.43, fax 02.40.02.43.55, e-mail eguitteny@aol.com
Tasting: by appt.**

COMTE DE LAUDONNIERE
Chardonnay 2002☆
20 hectares   70,000 bottles

Wine merchants Vinival offer this pale-yellow wine with its range of aromas. Fresh, balanced and persistently flavourful.

**SARL Vinival, La Sablette, 44330 Mouzillon,
tel. 02.40.36.66.00, fax 02.40.33.95.81**

DOMAINE BRUNO CORMERAIS
Elevé en Fût de Chêne 2001☆☆
0.8 hectares 3,000 bottles

A wine assembled from Cabernet Franc, Sauvignon, and Abouriou grape varieties and developed in cask over nine months. The last-named grape variety, from the southwest, is reputed to yield well-balanced wines; this 2001 is a fine example, not least by virtue of its deep-red colour and spicy aromas. The attack is smooth and accompanied by toasted notes, leading to a harmonious and balanced finish.

EARL Bruno et Marie-Françoise Cormerais,
La Chambaudière, 44190 Saint-Lumine-de-Clisson,
tel. 02.40.03.85.84, fax 02.40.06.68.74
Tasting: by appt.

 € 5-8

DOMAINE DE LA COUCHETIERE
Grolleau 2002☆
1.5 hectares   18,000 bottles

The de la Couchetière estate at Notre-Dame-d'Allençon boasts a range of agricultural produce, but viticulture started to predominate as of the 1980s. An attractive cellar reveals a seductive Grolleau with intense aromas of red fruit, notably cherries. Fresh and slightly tart, this 2002 boasts ample tannins and could benefit from cellaring for a further year before being served as an accompaniment to red meat.

GAEC Brault, Dom. de la Couchetière, 49380 Notre-Dame-d'Allençon,
tel. 02.41.54.30.26, fax 02.41.54.40.98
Tasting: ev. day except Sun. 8.30am–12.30pm 2.30pm–7pm

 € -3

DOMAINE DE LA COUPERIE
Cuvée Clyan Cabernet
Elevé en Fût de Chêne 2001☆☆ 🏆

2 hectares   6,000 bottles

The care that has gone into the production of this 2001 is evident from the very first sip. Impeccable cask maturation has spawned a subtle mix of vanilla, cinnamon and even cocoa aromas. The wine is harmonious on the palate, with silky tannins.

**EARL Claude Cogné, La Couperie, 49270 Saint-Christophe-la-Couperie, tel. 02.40.83.73.16, fax 02.40.83.76.71
Tasting: by appt.**

     € 3-5

LA COUR DE BLOIS
Cabernet Vieilli en Fût de Chêne 2001☆

1 hectare   5,300 bottles

This estate was totally revamped in 1985 with the planting of noble grape varieties, and Christelle and Thierry Brangeon go to great lengths to produce premium-quality wine. The dark-red body of this Cabernet 2001 presages a wine that has a fruity nose and works well on the palate. Wood aromas are still evident, but the wine is suited to being laid down over several years. The aromatic Gamay rosé (3–5 euros) also held the jury's interest.

**Christelle et Thierry Brangeon,
La Cour de Blois, 49270 Saint-Christophe-la-Couperie,
tel. 02.40.83.77.04, fax 02.40.83.77.05
Tasting: ev. day except Sun. 3pm–7pm**

    € 5-8

DOMAINE DE L'ERRIERE
Cabernet 2002☆

2.26 hectares   10,000 bottles

This thirty-two-hectare estate is located in the commune of Landreau in the Loire Atlantique. Two Cabernets contribute to a wine that deserves to be cellared for a number of years: an intensely flowery nose, sustained balance, and pronounced red fruit aromas combine to make this a most successful vintage.

GAEC Madeleineau Père et Fils, Dom. de L'Errière,
44430 Le Landreau,
tel. 02.40.06.43.94, fax 02.40.06.48.82
Tasting: by appt.

DOMAINE DE FLINES
Grolleau 2002☆

1.88 hectares   20,000 bottles

Chantal Motheron's family came originally from Touraine and has been involved in winemaking since the eighteenth century. As of the end of the 1960s it extended its operations in the Anjou region. Forty-year-old Grolleau vines underpin this attractive and sprightly wine, with its complex nose and intense aromas of spicy red fruit. Full and well-balanced, this should prove an ideal accompaniment to grilled meat.

C. Motheron, Dom. de Flines, 102, rue d'Anjou,
49540 Martigné-Briand,
tel. 02.41.59.42.78, fax 02.41.59.45.60
Tasting: by appt.

DOMAINE DU FOUR A CHAUX
L'Anthocyane 2000☆
5 hectares   13,000 bottles

Visitors to the estate can admire the newly renovated
eponymous whitewashed oven; they will also admire this
Anthocyane 2000 comprising 60% Cabernet Sauvignon
and 40% Cot grape varieties, with its intensely red robe
with mauve highlights and notes of peony. Fruit flavours
flood the palate, together with softened tannins. This is
a balanced wine which can be drunk now or laid down
for one to two years.

**EARL Dominique Norguet, Berger, 41100 Thoré-la-Rochette,
tel. 02.54.77.12.52, fax 02.54.80.23.22
Tasting: ev. day except Sun. 8am–12pm 2pm–7.30pm**

 €3-5

DOMAINE LA FRAIRIE DE LA MOINE
Gamay 2002☆
1 hectare   2,300 bottles

This 18.5 hectare vineyard extends along the banks of the
Moine only a few kilometres distant from the medieval city of
Clisson. The Gamay grape variety yields a pale rosé 2002 which
develops notes of fruit, notably raspberry and cherry. The clean
attack builds towards a wine that is balanced and pleasant.

**Hubert Chapeleau, La Garnière, 49230 Saint-Crespin-sur-Moine,
tel. 02.41.70.41.55, fax 02.41.70.49.44
Tasting: ev. day except Sun. 9am–12 noon 2pm–7pm**

 €-3

DOMAINE DES GILLIERES
Pays de Retz Grolleau 2002☆
9.02 hectares   100,000 bottles

This Pays de Retz Grolleau 2002 is macerated briefly on the skins; it comes into its own in the glass, where it gives off delicate notes of very ripe red fruit (cherry, gooseberry) that are echoed on a smooth and delicate palate, where hints of peach and apricot intrude. Best served with cold cuts.

Dominique Régnier, SAS des Gillières, 44690 La Haye-Fouassière, tel. 02.40.54.80.05, fax 02.40.54.89.56
Tasting: by appt.

    € .3

DOMAINE DU GRAND FIEF
Cuvée Prestige Chardonnay 2002☆☆
3.2 hectares   15,000 bottles

This straw-yellow Chardonnay 2002 exudes fruit aromas underpinned by floral notes. A voluminous and elegantly fresh wine with flavours of mango and peach: quite simply, an aperitif for all seasons.

EARL Dominique Guérin, Les Corbeillères, 44330 Vallet, tel. 02.40.36.27.37, fax 02.40.36.27.16
Tasting: ev. day except Sun. 8am–8pm

        € 5-8

DOMAINE DU GRAND LOGIS
Sauvignon 2002☆
2 hectares   4,000 bottles

In the seventeenth century, a seigneurial domaine stood on the site of this thirty-five-hectare estate. The Sauvignon grape variety yields this archetypal 2002, with notes of boxwood and supple and lingering flavours on the palate that make it an obvious and ideal companion to seafood.

EARL Lebrin, L'Aujardière, 44430 La Remaudière,
tel. 02.40.33.72.72, fax 02.40.33.74.18,
e-mail earl.lebrin@wanadoo.fr
Tasting: by appt.

 €.3

DOMAINE LES HAUTES NOELLES
Grolleau 2002☆
1.5 hectares   10,000 bottles

This expressive Grolleau 2002 comes from a small vineyard some ten kilometres from the lake of Grand-Lieu. Its lively red robe with violet highlights opens on a nose of aromas of very ripe red-berries (cherry) and a slightly amylic note. The fruitiness persists on the palate, where blackcurrant flavours predominate against a backdrop of soft tannins. A fresh and fruity wine which deserves to be drunk as of now.

Serge Batard, La Haute Galerie, 44710 Saint-Léger-les-Vignes,
tel. 02.40.31.53.49, fax 02.40.04.87.80,
e-mail sb.lhn@free.fr
Tasting: by appt.

 € 3-5

DOMAINE DE LA HOUSSAIS
Marches de Bretagne Cabernet 2001☆

1.5 hectares 9,000 bottles

Characteristic pepper notes blend with spice and smoked aromas in this 2001 Marches de Bretagne Cabernet. Good tannins and overall balance suggest this typical wine may need two more years to express its full potential.

Bernard Gratas, Dom. de La Houssais, 44430 Le Landreau, tel. 02.40.06.46.27, fax 02.40.06.47.25
Tasting: by appt.

    € 3-5

DOMAINE DE L'IMBARDIERE
Cabernet 2002☆

3.2 hectares 10,000 bottles

A deep-red wine with violet highlights typical of the Cabernet grape. The nose gives off ripe fruit and the body opens rich and harmonious on the palate.

Joseph Abline, L'Imbardière, 49270 Saint-Christophe-la-Couperie, tel. 02.40.83.90.62, fax 02.40.83.74.02, e-mail abline49vins@aol.com
Tasting: by appt.

 € -3

MANOIR DE L'HOMMELAIS
Gamay 2002☆☆
1.5 hectares   16,000 bottles

A weekend in the Nantes region is incomplete without a visit
to Dominique Brossard's remarkable *manoir*, where he will
tempt you with this Gamay Rosé 2002 that exudes remarkable
aromas of melon, pear and boiled sweets. The wine is fresh
and delicate on the palate, with overtones of mixed and citrus
fruits. A wine to be savoured in the company of close friends.
His blackcurrant-perfumed 2002 Rouge de Cabernet is a full
and powerful wine which deserves to be laid down.

Dominique Brossard, Manoir de l'Hommelais,
44310 Saint-Philbert-de-Grand-Lieu,
tel. 02.40.78.96.75, fax 02.40.78.76.91
Tasting: by appt.

DOMAINE DU MOULIN
Chardonnay 2002☆
2.6 hectares   2,000 bottles

This twenty-one-hectare, family run estate near the lake
of Grand-Lieu boasts the remains of an eighteenth century
mill that features on the label of this typically clear, yellow
Chardonnay, with its persistent fruit aromas developing into
a slightly tart yet charming finish.

Michel Figureau, Dom. du Moulin, 5, rue du Plessis,
44860 Pont-Saint-Martin,
tel. 02.40.32.70.56, fax 02.40.02.12.26,
e-mail figureau-michel@wanadoo.fr
Tasting: by appt.

LE MOULIN DE LA TOUCHE
Pays de Retz Grolleau 2002☆

2 hectares   8,000 bottles

Centres of local interest fringe this estate – the Museum of Retz two kilometres away, a vantage point from which to look over the salt marshes and out to sea, an eighteenth century windmill perched on a hillside, and – not least – this attractively rounded Rosé Grolleau 2002, all fruit and citrus flavours. Drunk with cold cuts or grilled meat, it will bring back pleasant memories of summer holidays.

Joël Hérissé, Le Moulin de la Touche, 44580 Bourgneuf-en-Retz, tel. 02.40.21.47.89, fax 02.40.21.47.89
Tasting: by appt.

PANNIER
Chardonnay 2002☆

71.46 hectares   857,600 bottles

This Chardonnay 2002 is distinguished by its golden colour and its flavours of almond and dried fruit and nuts. A fleshy and well-balanced palate makes it a most attractive table companion. A star also goes to the estate's Chenin 2002, with its green highlights, nuanced aromas of white flowers and its full-bodied, long finish.

Rémy Pannier, rue Léopold-Palustre, 49426 Saint-Hilaire-Saint-Florent, tel. 02.41.53.03.10, fax 02.41.53.03.19,
e-mail contact@remy-pannier.com
Tasting: ev. day 9am–12 noon 2pm–6pm

DOMAINE DU PARC
Pays de Retz Grolleau 2002☆☆

5 hectares   40,000 bottles

An attractive pink tinges the light and lustrous body of this
Grolleau 2002, with its citrus fruit (lemon) aromas which
mingle on the palate in a mix that is both fresh and fully
rounded; can be drunk now with fish or grilled meat. The
estate's Vin de Pays du Jardin de la France Chardonnay 2002
is also worth a mention.

**EARL Pierre Dahéron, Dom. du Parc, 44650 Corcoué-sur-Logne,
tel. 02.40.05.86.11, fax 02.40.05.94.98
Tasting: by appt.**

   € 5-8

LA PERRIERE
Chardonnay 2002☆

3 hectares   15,000 bottles

The La Perrière estate is situated in Pallet, a commune that
also has a reputation for quality Muscadets. The Chardonnay
2002 is golden in colour and exudes very delicate aromas.
Fleshy, fruity and fresh, it can be confidently predicted to age
into an elegant wine.

**Vincent Loiret, Ch. La Perrière, 44330 Le Pallet,
tel. 02.40.80.43.24, fax 02.40.80.46.99, e-mail viloiret@wanadoo.fr
Tasting: ev. day except Sun. 8am–12 noon 2pm–6pm; cl. 10–20 Aug.**

  € 3-5

DOMAINE PETIT CHATEAU
Chardonnay 2002☆☆

7 hectares   80,000 bottles

A pre-Revolution château at La Ragotière lends its name to this sixty-seven-hectare vineyard with its bourgeois manor. The tasting panel found this light Chardonnay 2002 typically supple and rounded, with a pleasantly fresh finish. The Couillaud brothers also showed two further Chardonnays which were noted by the jury, a Domaine Couillaud 2002 and the Domaine la Morinière 2002.

Couillaud Frères, Ch. Ragotière, La Regrippière, 44330 Vallet,
tel. 02.40.33.60.56, fax 02.40.33.61.89,
e-mail frères.couillaud@wanadoo.fr
Tasting: ev. day except Sat. Sun. 8am–12 noon 2pm–6pm

  € 5-8

DOMAINE DE PIERRE BLANCHE
Sauvignon 2002☆

1.4 hectares   6,000 bottles

This pale-yellow Sauvignon 2002 with green tones comes from a forty-hectare vineyard. It has a delicate and elegant nose, which translates on the palate to an attack that is lively and persistent. A fine example of this vintage.

EARL Vignoble Lecointre, Ch. La Tomaze, 6, rue du Pineau,
49380 Champ-sur-Layon,
tel. 02.41.78.86.34, fax 02.41.78.61.60
Tasting: by appt.

 € 5-8

DOMAINE DES PRIES
Pays de Retz Grolleau 2002☆

2.5 hectares   8,000 bottles

Exposure to the spray coming off the Atlantic Ocean and the presence of a sand and gravel soil contribute to the pleasant character of this Grolleau 2002. This is a fruity wine – raspberry, gooseberry, and strawberry – that has a lively and slightly tart taste. The Chardonnay 2002 du Pays de Retz was also noted by the jury.

Gérard Padiou, Les Priés, 44580 Bourgneuf-en-Retz,
tel. 02.40.21.45.16, fax 02.40.21.47.48
Tasting: by appt.

    € 3-5

DOMAINE DES QUATRE ROUTES
Gamay 2002☆

0.69 hectares   8,000 bottles

A relatively sustained salmon-pink hue is a feature of this Gamay 2002, as is its delicate perfume of spring flowers and citrus fruits underpinned by mineral notes. The wine continues fruity on the palate (strawberries) and has an appealing freshness. A wine to quench one's thirst and to accompany smoked salmon, salads, and cold cuts.

Dom. Henri Poiron et Fils, Les Quatre Routes,
44690 Maisdon-sur-Sèvre,
tel. 02.40.54.60.58, fax 02.40.54.62.05,
e-mail poiron.henri@wanadoo.fr
Tasting: by appt.

   € 3-5

MICHEL ROBINEAU
Sauvignon 2002☆☆

0.32 hectares   1,600 bottles

Citrus fruits and touches of blackcurrant announce a
Sauvignon 2002 that opens cleanly and continues to taste
fresh and fruity on the palate. The domaine's 2002 Rouge
de Grolleau also attracted the jury's attention.

Michel Robineau, 3, chem. du Moulin, Les Grandes Tailles,
49750 Saint-Lambert-du-Lattay,
tel. 02.41.78.34.67
Tasting: by appt.

    € 3-5

DOMAINE DE ROCHANVIGNE
Sauvignon 2002☆

1.28 hectares   10,000 bottles

In days gone by it was quite common in the area between
the Loire-Atlantique and the Vendée to come upon small
farm vineyards whre wine was produced exclusively for
family consumption. The tradition has been maintained
in this instance with the development of an honest and
fruity Sauvignon 2002, redolent of peaches and ripe pears,
that would go well with a fillet of fish in a white butter sauce.

Yann Corcessin, Le Plessis, 44116 Vieillevigne,
tel. 02.51.43.92.95, fax 02.51.43.92.95
Tasting: by appt.

     € 5-8

DOMAINE DE LA ROCHERIE
Cabernet Vieilli en Fût de Chêne 2001☆

2 hectares   10,000 bottles

This very typical Cabernet offers excellent value for money.
The merest hint of wood precedes aromas of red-berries
against a background of relatively supple tannins. Good
with red meat and cheese.

**Daniel Gratas, La Rocherie, 44430 Le Landreau,
tel. 02.40.06.41.55, fax 02.40.06.48.92
Tasting: ev. day except Sun. 8am–8pm**

CAVE DE LA ROUILLERE
Chardonnay 2002☆

16 hectares   150,000 bottles

A typical Chardonnay: pale yellow in colour with green
highlights, and a powerful nose with exotic nuances. This
is a wine that is not only supple but also fresh and sufficiently
aromatic as to make an excellent companion to grilled fish
or fish served with a sauce. The Chardonnay Cuvée Gaston
Rolandeau 2002 is also recommended.

**Les Vendangeoirs du Val de Loire, La Frémonderie, 49230 Tillières,
tel. 02.41.70.45.93, fax 02.41.70.43.74,
e-mail vvl@rolandeau.fr**

DOMAINE DE LA VIAUDIERE
Sauvignon 2002☆
1.5 hectares   8,000 bottles

The wine has a distinct hint of blackcurrant; it develops well on the palate into a most agreeable finish worthy of a first-rate example of this vintage.

**Giovannoni, EARL Vignoble Gélineau, la Viaudière,
49380 Champ-sur-Layon,
tel. 02.41.78.86.27, fax 02.41.78.60.45,
e-mail gelineau@wanadoo.fr
Tasting: ev. day except Sun. 9am–12.30pm 2pm–6pm**

      € 3-5

WINES SELECTED BUT NOT STARRED

DESTINEA
Sauvignon 2002
110,000 bottles

**SA Joseph Mellot, rte de Ménétréol, BP 13, 18300 Sancerre
tel. 02.48.78.54.54, fax 02.48.78.54.55
e-mail alexandremellot@josephmellot.com
Tasting: ev. day 8am–12 noon 1.30pm–5pm; Sat. Sun. by appt.**

    € 5-8

DOM. DE LA HALLOPIERE
Chardonnay 2002
20 hectares   100,000 bottles

**Vignerons des Terroirs de la Noëlle, Bd des Alliers, BP 155
44154 Ancenis Cedex,
tel. 02.40.98.92.72, fax 02.40.98.96.70
e-mail vignerons-noelle@cana.fr
Tasting: by appt.**

     € 3-5

Aquitaine and Charentes

The Aquitaine and Charentes region virtually encircles the city of Bordeaux and comprises the *départements* of Charente and Charente-Maritime, Gironde, Landes, Dordogne, and Lot-et-Garonne. The majority of the wines are supple, aromatic reds produced in the Aquitaine using Bordeaux grape varieties complemented by a few somewhat rustic local grapes such as Tannat, Abouriou, Bouchales, and Fer. Charente, Charente-Maritime, and Dordogne produce, in the main, white *vins de pays* that might be fine and light (Ugni Blanc, Colombard), rounded (Sémillon blends) or robust (Baroque). Charentais, Agenais, Terroirs Landais, and Thézac-Perricard are sub-regional designations, whereas Dordogne, Gironde, and Landes are *département*-based denominations.

DOMAINE DE BORDES
Moelleux 2002☆
1 hectare   6,600 bottles

Christian Morel, who also produces his own brand of armagnac, inherited this traditional family estate twenty years ago. His Moelleux 2002 is a clear straw-yellow wine distinguished by a strong attack. Complex aromas of citrus fruits underpin a liveliness that tempers the pronounced overall sweetness.

Christian Morel, Dom. de Bordes, 47170 Sainte-Maure-de-Peyriac, tel. 05.53.65.62.16, fax 05.53.65.21.63
Tasting: ev. day 8.30am–7pm except Sun. by appt.

 € 5-8

DOMAINE DE CAZEAUX
Cuvée Tradition 2001☆☆
8 hectares   4,000 bottles

An elegant label for a clear garnet-coloured wine which has been cask-matured to develop attractive aromatic notes, without eclipsing the flavours of pepper and violets. The aromas continue on the palate and remain delightful through to a long finish with persistent notes of undergrowth.

Eric Kauffer, Dom. de Cazeaux, 47170 Lannes, tel. 05.53.65.73.03, fax 05.53.65.88.95, e-mail domainecazeaux@free.fr
Tasting: by appt.

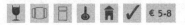 € 5-8

INSTANT CHOISI
Merlot-Cabernet Fruit Rouge☆

10 hectares   30,000 bottles

Clear and lively colour, small red-berry flavours. The wine opens strongly, reveals a balanced structure, with flavours of brandied fruits, and closes on a persistently smokey finish.

**Cave des Sept Monts, ZAC de Mondésir, 47150 Monflanquin,
tel. 05.53.36.33.40, fax 05.53.36.44.11
Tasting: ev. day 9am–12.30pm 3pm–6.30pm**

  €-3

DOMAINE LOU GAILLOT
Merlot Excellence 2001☆

1 hectare   6,000 bottles

This is a lustrous ruby wine and its principal appeal lies in its bold attack and its full and fleshy impact on the palate. Gentle tannins blend smoothly with well-integrated wood notes.

**Gilles Pons, Les Gaillots, 47440 Casseneuil,
tel. 05.53.41.04.66, fax 05.53.01.13.89
Tasting: ev. day except Sun. 9am–12.30pm 2pm–7.30pm**

 €5-8

WINE SELECTED BUT NOT STARRED

DOM. DE CAMPET
Grain d'Automne Gros Manseng 2001

2.4 hectares   2,600 bottles

**Carole et Joël Buisson, SCEA de Campet, 47170 Sos,
tel. 05.53.65.63.60, fax 05.53.65.36.79
Tasting: by appt. cl. Feb.**

    €5-8

CHARENTAIS

BRARD BLANCHARD 2002☆

1.6 hectares   16,600 bottles

Merlot, Cabernet Franc, Sauvignon, and Malbec come together
in this vineyard, which has operated along organic lines for
thirty years. This 2002 has a fruity nose and opens round,
subtle and well-balanced on the palate, providing an excellent
accompaniment to cold cuts and meat.

GAEC Brard Blanchard, 1, chem. de Routreau, Boutiers,
16100 Cognac,
tel. 05.45.32.19.58, fax 05.45.36.53.21
Tasting: ev. day except Sun. 9am–12 noon 2pm–6pm;
Sat. 9am–12 noon

 € 3-5

DOMAINE BRUNEAU
Sauvignon 2002☆

1 hectare   8,000 bottles

The hills and valleys of Rouffignac are a rambler's paradise.
Alain Pillet's small domaine in Rouffignac produces a well-
balanced Sauvignon which gives off fresh aromas that will
perfectly complement seafood platters and even poultry.

Alain Pillet, chez Bruneau, 17130 Rouffignac,
tel. 05.46.49.04.82, fax 05.46.70.07.95
Tasting: by appt.

 € 3-5

CHAI DU ROUISSOIR
Cabernet Terroir de Fossiles 2002☆
1 hectare   1,500 bottles

Didier Chapon and his son Hugues have been producing *vins de pays* since 1996. Together, they have developed this attractive and elegant rosé which appeals both to the eye and the palate. Recommended to be served on its own as an aperitif, or as an accompaniment to cold cuts.

Chapon, Roussillon, Chai du Rouissoir, 17500 Ozillac,
tel. 05.46.48.14.76, fax 05.46.48.14.76,
e-mail chaidurouissoir@hotmail.com
Tasting: ev. day except Sun. 10am–12 noon 5pm–7pm

 € 3-5

DOMAINE DE LA CHAUVILLIERE
Chardonnay 2002☆☆
10 hectares   40,000 bottles

A Chardonnay 2002 that opens with intense aromas of citrus fruits and sustains flavours through to a persistent finish. Should be drunk with fish dishes and seafood – all the more so since the oyster beds of the Marennes lie only twenty kilometres distant.

EARL Hauselmann et Fils, Dom. de La Chauvillière,
17600 Sablonceaux,
tel. 05.46.94.44.40, fax 05.46.94.44.63
Tasting: by appt.

 € 5-8

DOMAINE GARDRAT
Colombard 2002☆☆

4.8 hectares   47,000 bottles

Jean-Pierre Gardrat tends to this twenty-eight-hectare vineyard on the slopes of the Gironde, carrying on a family tradition dating back to the close of the eighteenth century. His Colombard 2002 gives off aromas of mango and passion-fruit which pre-empt an elegant and balanced palate. Can be taken as an aperitif or drunk throughout a meal.

Jean-Pierre Gardrat, La Touche, 17120 Cozes,
tel. 05.46.90.86.94, fax 05.46.90.95.22,
e-mail lionel.gardrat@wanadoo.fr
Tasting: by appt.

 € 3-5

DOMAINE DU GROLLET
Merlot-Cabernet Sauvignon 2001☆

20.1 hectares   30,000 bottles

The celebrated Cognac producer Rémy-Martin has converted 20 hectares of this 200-hectare estate to the production of *vins de pays*. This 2002 is a harmonious wine which will mature into an agreeable accompaniment to meat dishes.

SA Les Dom. Rémy-Martin, 29, rue de la Société-Vinicole, BP 37,
16100 Cognac,
tel. 05.45.35.76.00, fax 05.45.35.77.94

     € 3-5

MOINE FRERES
Chenin 2002☆

1.92 hectares   1,700 bottles

Jean-Yves et François Moine offer a conducted tour of Chêne that enables visitors to the domaine to learn something of the skills that go into oak-splitting and barrel-making. Their lively Chenin 2002 boasts pleasant notes of refreshing citrus and goes best with seafood.

SNC Jean-Yves et François Moine, Villeneuve, 16200 Chassors, tel. 05.45.80.98.91, fax 05.45.80.96.01, e-mail lesfreres.moine@wanadoo.fr
Tasting: by appt.

LE ROYAL
Ile de Ré 2002☆

25 hectares   240,000 bottles

Fish dishes and seafood platters are the order of the day in the case of this likeable Chardonnay – typical of the Ile de Ré – which comprises roughly equal parts of Sauvignon, Chardonnay and Colombard.

Coop. des Vignerons de l'Ile de Ré, 17580 Le Bois-Plage-en-Ré, tel. 05.46.09.23.09, fax 05.46.09.09.26
Tasting: by appt.

SORNIN
Cabernet Sauvignon-Merlot Cuvée Privilège Elevé en Fût 2001☆

3.7 hectares   29,000 bottles

An eight-month maturation in oak barrels yields this well-rounded and very aromatic Cuvée Privilège, that deserves a regular place at the family table.

**SCA Cave de Saint-Sornin, Les Combes, 16220 Saint-Sornin,
tel. 05.45.23.92.22, fax 05.45.23.11.61,
e-mail contact@cavesaintsornin.com
Tasting: ev. day except Sun. 8am–12 noon 2pm–6pm**

 € 3-5

ST A.
Merlot 2001☆

5 hectares   13,000 bottles

From co-op cellars dating from 1999 comes this fruity and well-rounded Merlot 2001. A wine that is ready to be drunk with meat dishes and specialties of the Charentes region.

**Cave Coop. ACV, ZI du Malestier, 16130 Ségonzac,
tel. 05.45.36.48.38, fax 05.45.36.48.36,
e-mail cave.acv@wanadoo.fr
Tasting: by appt.**

 € 5-8

TERRA SANA 2002☆☆

17 hectares   130,000 bottles

Organically cultivated. A blend of Ugni Blanc, Sauvignon Blanc, and Colombard, fruit flavours assail the nose while the wine is fine and subtle on the palate. Good with seafood.

SA Jacques et François Lurton, Dom. de Poumeyrade, 33870 Vayres, tel. 05.57.55.12.12, fax 05.57.55.12.13, e-mail jflurton@jflurton.com

    € 5-8

LANDES

FLEUR DES LANDES
Cabernet-Tannat 2002☆

6 hectares   50,000 bottles

This supple, rounded wine is deep in colour and pleasant on the nose. An added attraction is its colourful floral label.

Vins Duprat Frères, quai Pièce-Noyée, chem. St-Bernard, 64100 Bayonne, tel. 05.59.55.65.65, fax 05.59.55.41.52, e-mail vins.duprat@wanadoo.fr Tasting: ev. day except Sat. Sun. 8am–12 noon 2pm–5pm

      € 3-5

WINE SELECTED BUT NOT STARRED

DOM. D'ESPERANCE
Cuvée d'Or 2002

12 hectares   16,000 bottles

Claire de Montesquiou, Dom. d'Espérance, 40240 Mauvezin-d'Armagnac, tel. 05.58.44.85.93, e-mail info@espérance.com.fr Tasting: by appt.

    € 3-5

VIN DE DOMME
Tradition 2002☆

5 hectares   22,000 bottles

This cooperative has emerged as a proactive force in the rebirth of Périgord Noir winemaking, following the decimation of vineyards in the region by phylloxera. A walk through the countryside offers visitors an opportunity to see the original wine-worker cabins of dry stone, with their cone-shaped lauze-tiled roofs. The Domme Tradition 2002 is distinguished by a rich-red colour and pungent aromas of preserved red fruit with pronounced mineral notes – the distinctive signature, as it were, of this type of wine. On the palate, the wine lives up to expectations in terms of both volume and robustness. That said, the tasting panel would have appreciated a longer finish. An interesting wine that is well worth discovering.

**Les Vignerons des Coteaux du Céou, Moncalou,
24200 Florimont-Gaumier,
tel. 05.53.28.14.47, fax 05.53.28.32.48,
e-mail vignerons-du-ceou@wanadoo.fr
Tasting: by appt.**

   € 5-8

TERROIRS LANDAIS

ROUGE DE BACHEN 2001 ☆☆ ♈

10 hectares   15,500 bottles

Starred chefs regularly feel the temptation to try their hand
at winemaking: Blanc, Meneau, Lorain have done so and now so
too Michel Guérard with this 80% Merlot and 20% Tannat
2001 blend produced on ten hectares of a twenty-hectare estate.
He is to be complimented on a wine that boasts a shimmering
colour, a fine and full wood-flavoured nose, and a full and fruity
palate – suitable, in short, to grace the best of tables.

Michel Guérard, Cie Hôtelière et Fermière d'Eugénie-les-Bains,
Ch. de Bachen, 40800 Duhort-Bachen,
tel. 05.58.71.76.76, fax 05.58.71.77.77,
e-mail michel.guerard@wanadoo.fr
Tasting: by appt.

 € 11-15

COTEAUX DE CHALOSSE 2002 ☆

6 hectares   50,000 bottles

Cabernet (70%) and Tannat (30%) varieties go into the
making of this attractively coloured wine, whose nose is
discreet but unambiguous. This 2002 is rounded on the palate
and leaves a distinct impression of fullness. The jury also
awarded a star each to the estate's Vins de Pays des Landes
Rouge Gailande 2002 and a rosé 2002.

Les Vignerons Landais, 40320 Geaune,
tel. 05.58.44.51.25, fax 05.58.44.40.22,
e-mail info@vlandais.com
Tasting: ev. day except Sun. 9am–12 noon 2pm–5.30pm

 € 3-5

DOMAINE DE LABALLE
Sables Fauves 2002☆
12 hectares   40,000 bottles

Dominique Laudet was a Gascon gentleman who spent some time in America before acquiring this estate in 1820. The estate has remained in the family ever since, producing armagnac (of course) but, as of 1982, also wine. Colombard, Gros Manseng and Ugni Blanc (60, 30, and 10% respectively) go into this pale gold 2002, with its pungent aromas of confectionery and acacia blossom. Alcohol content and acidity are well-balanced and there is a hint of residual sugar which is by no means unpleasant. A wine made for foie gras perhaps? The jury also selected a Chardonnay des Landes 2002.

SCEA Noël et Christian Laudet, Le Moulin de Laballe, 40310 Parleboscq,
tel. 05.58.44.33.39, fax 05.58.44.92.61,
e-mail n.laudet@wanadoo.fr
Tasting: ev. day except Sat. Sun. 8am–5pm

DOMAINE DU TASTET
Coteaux de Chalosse 2002☆
5,000 bottles

A Coteaux de Chalosse developed from a blend of Cabernet Franc (80%) and Tannat grape varieties, this liquorice-tasting red develops aromas of red fruit accompanied by elegant tannins. The tasting jury also selected the estate's moderately priced Gros Manseng Moelleux 2002.

EARL J.-C. Romain et Fils, Dom. du Tastet, 2350, chem. d'Aymont,
40350 Pouillon,
tel. 05.58.98.28.27, fax 05.58.98.27.63,
e-mail domaine-tastet@voila.fr
Tasting: by appt.

DOM. D'AUGERON

Sables Fauves 2002

7 hectares   4,200 bottles

**Régine Bubola, Dom. d'Augeron, 40190 Le Frèche,
tel. 05.58.45.82.30, fax 05.58.03.13.81,
e-mail domaine.augeron@wanadoo.fr
Tasting: ev. day except Sun. 8am–12 noon 2pm–6pm**

  €3-5

DOM. DE CAMENTRON

Sables de l'Océan Cabernet Franc 2002

1 hectares   6,000 bottles

**Bouyrie-Dutirou, SCEA Les Vignes de Camentron, chem. de Camentron,
40660 Messanges, tel. 05.58.48.83.81, fax 05.58.48.92.30
Tasting: by appt. Prop: Bouyrie-Dutirou**

   €5-8

THEZAC-PERRICARD

VIN DU TSAR

Le Bouquet 2001☆

2.5 hectares   20,000 bottles

Red-fruit aromas and hints of game; with soft and fleshy
tannins that accompany a persistent and musky finish. The
Vin du Tsar Tradition 2001 was also picked out by the jury.

**Les Vignerons de Thézac-Perricard, Plaisance, 47370 Thézac,
tel. 05.53.40.72.76, fax 05.53.40.78.76,
e-mail info@vin-du-tsar.tm.fr
Tasting: ev. day 9.15am–12.15pm 2pm–6pm; Sun. 2pm–6pm**

   €3-5

The Garonne

With Toulouse at its heart, this region embraces the designation Vin de Pays du Comté Tolosan, that includes the following *départements*: Ariège, Aveyron, Haute-Garonne, Gers, Lot, Lot-et-Garonne, Pyrénées-Atlantiques, Hautes-Pyrénées, Tarn, and Tarn-et-Garonne. Sub-regions are Côtes du Tarn; Coteaux de Glanes (Haut-Quercy, to the north of Lot – reds worth ageing); Coteaux du Quercy (south of Cahors – structured reds); Saint-Sardos (left bank of the Garonne river); Coteaux et Terrasses de Montauban (light reds); Côtes de Gascogne, Côtes du Condomois, and Côtes de Montestruc (the armagnac-producing areas of Gers; mainly whites); and Bigorre. Haute-Garonne, Tarn-et-Garonne, Pyrénées-Atlantiques, Lot, Aveyron, and Gers are designations that correspond to *départements*.

Production is approximately 200,000 hectolitres red and rosé; 400,000 hectolitres white (in the Gers and Tarn). Soil and climatic variations here and along the Atlantic seaboard south of the Massif Central combine with a wide range of grape varieties. Accordingly, there is every incentive to develop wines made to a consistent standard that, as of 1982, have been labelled Vin de Pays du Comté Tolosan. But, at the time of writing, production remains comparatively low, at around 40,000 hectolitres from a total of some fifteen times greater for the region as a whole.

COMTE TOLOSAN

FRANCOIS DAUBERT
Madrigal sur le Mauzac 2001☆☆
0.6 hectares   1,500 bottles

Frontonnais vineyards are known above all for their output of red wines. That said, certain winemakers – and François Daubert is a case in point – have the expertise and know-how to produce viable whites. This Mauzac 2001, for example, has a vanilla nose, is perfectly balanced on the palate with rich aromas of pear, quince, and honey, and has a hint of wood that allows it to finish long and full-bodied.

François Daubert, Ch. Joliet, 345, chem. de Caillol, 31620 Fronton, tel. 05.61.82.46.02, fax 05.61.82.34.56, e-mail chateau.joliet@wanadoo.fr
Tasting: by appt.

 € 8-11

DOMAINE DE RIBONNET
Chardonnay-Sauvignon 2001☆☆ 🏆
6,500 bottles

Christian Gerber's Domaine de Ribonnet offers a wide range of *vins de pays*, each with its own forceful personality. The jury was particularly attracted to this Chardonnay-Sauvignon, with its delicate yet complex and distinctive nose and discreet hints of wood. The wine finishes long, full, and spicy on the palate. Top-of-the-range is the watchword in this instance – a truly Epicurean pleasure.

SARL Vallées et Terroirs, Dom. de Ribonnet, 31870 Beaumont-sur-Lèze, tel. 05.61.08.71.02, fax 05.61.08.08.06
Tasting: by appt.

 € 5-8

VIN DE FLEUR 2002 ☆

15 hectares   100,000 bottles

The Vin de Fleur range in white, rosé, and red from the Crouseilles cellars has long been synonymous with wines that are pleasingly full and that make for easy drinking. This predominantly Colombard-based 2002 literally glides across the tongue; its citrus fruit nose is pungent, and it is finely balanced and nuanced on the palate.

Cave de Crouseilles, 64350 Crouseilles, tel. 05.62.69.66.87, fax 05.62.69.62.71, e-mail m.darricau@plaimont.fr
Tasting: by appt.

     € -3

CORREZE

WINE SELECTED BUT NOT STARRED

MILLE ET UNE PIERRES
Elevé en Fût de Chêne 2001

15 hectares   100,000 bottles

Cave viticole de Branceilles, Le Bourg, 19500 Branceilles, tel. 05.55.84.09.01, fax 05.55.25.33.01, e-mail cave-viticole-de-branceilles@wanadoo.fr
Tasting: ev. day except Sun. 10am–12 noon 3pm–16pm

 € 5-8

COTEAUX ET TERRASSES DE MONTAUBAN

DOMAINE DE MONTELS
Louise 2001☆☆

2 hectares   10,000 bottles

Philippe and Thierry Romain offer a complete range of top-quality wines, among which the jury selected a Louise 2001 with a pungent nose of red-berries and violets. The wine opens strongly; the evolving tannins are as yet delicate, full, and well balanced, with notes of spice and quince. Lady Louise promises to be a delight.

Philippe et Thierry Romain, Dom. de Montels, 82350 Albias,
tel. 05.63.31.02.82, fax 05.63.31.07.94
Tasting: ev. day except Sun. 8am–12 noon 2pm–7pm

€ 5-8

COTES DU CONDOMOIS

PRESTIGE DU CONDOMOIS 2002☆

100,000 bottles

Les Terres de Gascogne yields red or rosé *vins de pays* that deserve to be better-known on account of their dominant aromas of peach and apricots and fresh, fruity, and well-balanced impact on the palate.

Vignoble de Gascogne, Cave de Condom, 32400 Riscle,
tel. 05.62.69.62.87, fax 05.62.69.66.71,
e-mail f.latapy@plaimont.fr
Tasting: by appt.

 € 3-5

DOMAINE LES ACACIAS
Petit Manseng 2002☆

1.5 hectares   6,700 bottles

An assortment of exotic fruit aromas (mango), with hints of white blossom. Fine and well-balanced. Discove and enjoyed.

Dom. les Acacias, GAEC Camp du Haut, 32310 Bezolles,
tel. 05.62.28.57.16, fax 05.62.28.57.16, e-mail gersmoutarde@aol.com
Tasting: ev. day 10.30am–12.30pm 4pm–7pm; Mon. Sun. by appt.
Prop: I. Dupouy et M. Delaère

    € 8-11

DOMAINE LE BOUSCAS
Merlot 2001☆

1 hectare   6,000 bottles

An exquisite ruby-robed Merlot; with rounded, delicate aromas of ripe red fruit (notably strawberries), also on the palate.

Floréal Romero, Dom. le Bouscas, 32330 Gondrin,
tel. 05.62.29.11.87, fax 05.62.29.11.87, e-mail fromero@free.fr
Tasting: by appt.

   € 8-11

CAPRICE DE COLOMBELLE 2002☆

250,000 bottles

Beautiful yellow, with green highlights. Intense boxwood and exotic fruit aromas. Well-defined, balanced, long. Accomplished.

Producteurs Plaimont, 32400 Saint-Mont,
tel. 05.62.69.62.87, fax 05.62.69.61.68, e-mail f.latapy@plaimont.fr
Tasting: by appt.

   € 3-5

DOMAINE DES CASSAGNOLES
Gros Manseng Sélection 2002☆☆
6 hectares   40,000 bottles

J. and G. Baumann have contrived to bring out the best
in Gascon grape varieties across their comprehensive range
of *vins de pays*. The jury opted for this Gros Manseng 2002
with its sustained yellow-to-gold colour and green highlights.
The delicate mint aromas are complemented by hints of
preserved fruit, toast, and pear. The wine tastes of citrus
fruits and finishes long and structured.

J. et G. Baumann, Dom. des Cassagnoles,
EARL de la Ténarèze, 32330 Gondrin,
tel. 05.62.28.40.57, fax 05.62.28.42.42,
e-mail j.baumann@domainedescassagnoles.com
Tasting: ev. day except Sun. 9am–5.30pm

DOMAINE D'EMPEYRON 2001☆
10 hectares   5,000 bottles

The winemakers of Ténarèze may produce principally Côtes
de Gascogne whites, but they also offer a not inconsiderable
range of reds, including this Domaine d'Empeyron 2001 with
its intense fruit aromas, notably of slightly spicy strawberry
and plum, and gentle yet full and well-structured tannins
that round out on the palate.

Les Vignerons de la Ténarèze, rte de Mouchan, 32190 Vic-Fezensac,
tel. 05.62.58.05.25, fax 05.62.06.34.21
Tasting: by appt.

DOMAINE DE JOY
Sauvignon-Gros Manseng 2002☆☆☆
3 hectares 20,000 bottles

A perfect balance is achieved between the Sauvignon and Gros Manseng grape varieties in this 2002, where the hints of boxwood from the former are overlaid by the more complex citrus aromas of the latter variety. On the palate, this first impression is sustained, with boxwood flavours giving way to the more exotic and fleshy taste of the Gros Manseng, to ensure both length and body. Olivier and Roland Gessler are to be applauded for this skilful *assemblage* (blend) which brings out the best features of both grape varieties. This is a very, very good wine.

Olivier et Roland Gessler, Dom. de Joÿ, 32110 Panjas, tel. 05.62.09.03.20, fax 05.62.69.04.46, e-mail contact@domaine-joy.com
Tasting: ev. day except Sun. 9am–12.30pm 2pm–7pm

DOMAINE DE LARTIGUE 2001 ☆☆
3 hectares 6,600 bottles

This Côtes de Gascogne 2001 exhibits a deep-red body and is uncommonly rich in strong and complex aromas and floral, fruit and vegetable notes. The palate offers red fruits and nuances of fig, and is honest and balanced. The wine finishes full-bodied and long, as a complete red should.

Francis Lacave, Au Village, 32800 Bretagne-d'Armagnac, tel. 05.62.09.90.09, fax 05.62.09.79.60
Tasting: ev. day 8am–12.30pm 2pm–7pm

DOMAINE DES PERSENADES
Gros Manseng Moelleux 2002☆
1.1 hectares   10,000 bottles

White blossom and grapefruit, with surprising persistence of lightly vanilla-scented peach and apricot flavours. Fresh, with body and perfect balance.

Christian Marou, Dom. des Persenades, 32800 Cazeneuve, tel. 05.62.09.99.30, fax 05.62.09.84.64, e-mail marou@terre-net.fr Tasting: ev. day 8am–8pm

DOM. DU TARIQUET
Les Premières Grives 2002☆☆
85 hectares   1000,000 bottles

Straw-coloured with golden highlights; distinguished by powerful yet elegant mandarine, apricot, and vanilla aromas. Full, lively, and balanced on the palate, with honey, dried fruit, and prune. A must – as always.

SCV Ch. du Tariquet, 32800 Eauze tel. 05.62.09.87.82, fax 05.62.09.89.49, e-mail contact@tariquet.com Prop: Famille Grassa

WINE SELECTED BUT NOT STARRED

COLLIER DE LA TOISON D'OR 2002
32.5 hectares   350,000 bottles

La Fiée des Lois, 21, rue Montgolfier, BP 90022, 79232 Prahecq Cedex, tel. 05.49.32.15.15, fax 05.49.32.16.05, e-mail selection@fdlois.fr

DOMAINE DE LA HIGUERE
Cabernet Sauvignon-Merlot Cuvée Boisée 2001

17 hectares   20,000 bottles

**Paul et David Esquiro, Dom. de la Higuère, 32390 Mirepoix,
tel. 05.62.65.18.05, fax 05.62.65.13.80,
e-mail esquiro@free.fr**

   € 3-5

DOMAINE D'UBY
Colombard-Ugni Blanc 2002

20 hectares 20,000 bottles

**EARL Jean-Charles Morel, Uby, 32150 Cazaubon, tel. 05.62.09.51.93,
fax 05.62.09.58.94, e-mail domaineuby@wanadoo.fr
Tasting: by appt.**

   € 3-5

COTES DU TARN

DOMAINE SARRABELLE
Chardonnay 2001☆☆

1 hectare   6,000 bottles

This wine is from the range of single-grape Côtes du Tarn
from Laurent and Fabien Caussé. A slight but distinctive
sparkle gives freshness that is well-balanced and harmonious.

**Laurent et Fabien Caussé, Les Fortis, 81310 Lisle-sur-Tarn,
tel. 05.63.40.47.78, e-mail domaine-sarrabelle@free.fr
Tasting: ev. day except Sun. 8am–7pm**

       € 3-5

DOMAINE VIGNE LOURAC
Sauvignon Prestige 2002☆
3 hectares   30,000 bottles

Alain Gayrel has produced excellent Sauvignons for a long time
– and this wine is no exception to the rule. A powerfully floral
nose and intense fruit flavours impart a pleasing freshness.

**Vignobles Philippe Gayrel, BP 4, 81600 Gaillac,
tel. 05.63.81.21.05, fax 05.63.81.21.09**

   € -3

LES VIGNES DES GARBASSES
Syrah 2002☆☆
0.5 hectares   2,000 bottles

Brilliant and intense garnet colour. Elegant nose, with floral
aromas. Forceful tannins give volume and structure. Age well.

**Guy Fontaine, Le Bousquet, 81500 Cabanes,
tel. 05.63.42.02.05
Tasting: by appt.**

    € 5-8

WINE SELECTED BUT NOT STARRED

DOMAINE D'EN SEGUR
Cuvée Germain Elevé en Fût de Chêne 2000
43,694 bottles

**SCEA En Gourau-En Ségur, rte de Saint-Sulpice, 81500 Lavaur,
tel. 05.63.58.09.45, fax 05.63.58.09.45,
e-mail ensegur@terre-net.fr
Tasting: by appt. Prop: Pierre Fabre**

  € 5-8

LOT

DOMAINE DES ARDAILLOUX
Chardonnay Cuvée Tradition 2002☆☆☆

4.8 hectares   24,130 bottles

Brimming with individuality; pungent floral nose; full and long.

SCEA Ch. des Ardailloux, Les Ardailloux, 46700 Soturac,
tel. 05.53.71.30.45, e-mail ardailloux@aol.com
Tasting: ev. day 10am–6pm except Sat. Sun. Oct.–Apr.

  € 8-11

LOT-ET-GARONNE

COTEAUX DU MEZINAIS
Gros Manseng Moelleux 2002☆

0.9 hectares   8,000 bottles

Round and oaky, full-bodied with a long toasty finish.

Cave des Coteaux du Mézinais, 1, bd du Colome, 47170 Mézin,
tel. 05.53.65.53.55, e-mail cave.mezinais@wanadoo.fr
Tasting: by appt.

   € 3-5

SAINT-SARDOS

GILLES DE MORBAN 1999☆
90 hectares   120,000 bottles

Decidedly robust, pungent, with firm tannins. Fleshy and ample.

Cave des Vignerons de Saint-Sardos, Le Bourg, 82600 Saint-Sardos,
tel. 05.63.02.52.44, e-mail cave.saintsardos@free.fr
Tasting: by appt.

   € 3-5

Languedoc-Roussillon

The Languedoc-Roussillon region, shaped like some vast amphitheatre opening on the Mediterranean, is home to vineyards that extend from the Rhône down to the eastern Pyrénées. This region, the largest wine-growing area in all of France, produces close on eighty per cent of all *vins de pays*. Aude, Gard, Hérault, and Pyrénées-Orientales, the four designations that take their name from *départements*, yield a total of some 3.1 million hectolitres annually. Within each of these *départements*, *vins de pays* produced in more closely delineated zones (of which there are no fewer than fifty-seven) total around one million hectolitres.

Vin de Pays d'Oc, the regional designation, produces eighty per cent of the total annual 3.5-million-hectolitre yield from the six principal grape varieties (Cabernet Sauvignon, Merlot, and Syrah for reds and Chardonnay, Sauvignon, and Viognier for whites)

Vins de pays from the Languedoc-Roussillon are produced by individually fermenting selected harvests of traditional grape varieties (Carignan, Cinsault, Grenache, and Syrah for the reds and rosés, and Clairette, Grenache Blanc, Macabeu, Muscat, and Terret for the whites), together with varieties from other regions, notably Merlot, Cabernet Sauvignon, Cabernet Franc, Cot, Petit Verdot, and Pinot Noir for reds, and for whites, Chardonnay, Sauvignon, and Viognier.

DOMAINE DE LA BOUYSSE
Merlot 2001☆

1.5 hectares   4,730 bottles

Martine Pagès and Christophe Molinier have taken charge of the domaine once operated by their grandfather and have trebled the planted surface area (fifty hectares) and reconfigured it along biodynamic lines. This Merlot 2001 has a cherry hue with violet highlights; it opens very gently, giving off aromas of vanilla. The tannins are distinctly rounded in a wine full of character.

Dom. de la Bouysse, rue des Ecoles, 11200 Saint-André-de-Roquelongue, tel. 04.68.45.50.34, fax 04.68.45.09.86
Tasting: by appt.

    € 5-8

DOMAINE DE FONTENELLES
Cuvée du Poête Renaissance 2002☆

11 hectares   20,000 bottles

The Fontenelles domaine has been in the same family for five generations and runs to forty hectares in total. Meeting Thierry Tastu, Renaissance Man personified, is an experience not to be missed. A composer-poet who conjures up rare harmonies of Merlot and Grenache, and Syrah and Vieux Carignan, his luminous, darkly brooding Cuvée du Poête Renaissance, produced from eleven hectares, is a delight to the eye, to the nose – a complex mix of ripe fruit and chocolate – and to the palate, where it opens full and fleshy. A good wine.

Thierry Tastu, 78, av. des Corbières, 11700 Douzens,
tel. 04.67.58.15.27, fax 04.67.58.15.27,
e-mail t.tastu@montpellier.cci.fr
Tasting: by appt.

      € 5-8

BENOVIE

DOMAINE DES HOSPITALIERS
Merlot 2001☆
6,000 bottles

The eponymous "*hospitallers*" of the domaine name date back to the twelfth century Foundation of the Order of Hospitaliers of St John of Jerusalem. Today, the domaine boasts forty hectares in total. This Merlot 2001 is irreproachable in terms of colour, with a powerful nose redolent of gooseberries and with a hint of vanilla from the cask. The tannins are well-structured and the finish packs a punch.

Martin-Pierrat, Dom. des Hospitaliers, 34400 Saint-Christol, tel. 04.67.86.01.15, fax 04.67.86.00.19
Tasting: ev. day 8am–8pm

    € 5-8

CASSAN

DOMAINE SAINTE MARTHE
Syrah 2002☆
10 hectares   120,000 bottles

An attractively deep colour for this Syrah 2002, which develops delicate aromas of fruit. The wine shows balance and density. This is a "serious" Syrah that, provided it lives up to its early promise, deserves a "most honourable mention".

Olivier Bonfils, Dom. de Sainte-Marthe, 34320 Roujan, tel. 04.67.93.10.10, fax 04.67.93.10.05

    € 3-5

DOMAINE DE LA TOUR PENEDESSES
Tempranillo Mas de Couy
Elevé en Fût de Chêne 2001☆☆

3 hectares   8,000 bottles

Alexandre Fouque describes himself as an *"artisan-vigneron"*
on the label of this 2001. An oenologist by profession,
Fouque learned his craft in Champagne and Suze-la-Rousse.
His vat room is furnished with equipment from Burgundy.
A truly ecumenical winemaker, then, whose Tempranillo
brings tears to the eyes. This is a version of the celebrated
oeil-de-lièvre (eye of the hare) Rioja successfully transposed
to the Languedoc. Bouquet and body are full, warm, and
welcoming, with aromas of mature fruit. A wine to be
served at room temperature with small game pâté or a
tarte tatin.

**Dom. de La Tour Penedesses, rte de Fouzilhon, 34320 Gabian,
tel. 04.67.24.14.41, fax 04.67.24.14.22,
e-mail domainedelatourpenedesses@yahoo.fr
Tasting: by appt.**

 € 8-11

CATALAN

MAS BAUX
Grenache Noir Velours Rouge 2001☆☆
3.71 hectares   4,517 bottles

These alluvial terraces bordering the Via Domitia have been planted with vines since time immemorial and the Catalan mas by the roadside has been here since the sixteenth century. This Grenache Noir 2001 vintage, with its attractive fuchsia highlights, gives off aromas of minerals and ripe fruit in equal proportions. It is full-bodied, supple and velvet-like on the palate. Two stars each are also awarded to a Mas Baux Rouge-Gorge 2001 and a Mas Baux Rouge Baux 2001.

EARL Mas des Baux, Chem. du Mas Durand, 66140 Canet-en-Roussillon, tel. 04.68.80.25.04, fax 04.68.80.25.04, e-mail mariepierre.baux@libertysurf.fr
Tasting: by appt.

 € 11-15

DOMAINE MOSSE
Le Carignan 2001☆☆
3 hectares   3,500 bottles

An excellent example of the Carignan grape variety from century-old vine stock, this 2001 boasts a purple body with even deeper purple highlights and a nose that is laced with spices, liquorice, and preserved fruit. The wine opens strongly on the palate but maintains its essentially rounded character.

Jacques Mossé, Ch. Mossé, BP 8, 66301 Ste-Colombe-de-la-Commanderie, tel. 04.68.53.08.89, fax 04.68.53.35.13, e-mail chateau.mosse@worldonline.fr
Tasting: by appt.

 € 15-23

CATHARE

DOMAINE DE SAUTES
Signature Cathare 2002☆

3 hectares   30,000 bottles

This 2002 is a torch-bearer blend of Merlot (50%), Caladoc and Syrah and, as such, is a near-perfect wine: deep purple in colour, a pungent and well-developed nose, and supple and voluminous on the palate.

Guy et Emmanuel Giva, Dom. de Sautes, RN 113, 11000 Carcassonne, tel. 04.68.78.77.98, fax 04.68.78.51.66, e-mail domainedesautes@libertysurf.fr
Tasting: ev. day except Sun. 10am–12 noon 2pm–6pm

 € 3-5

CAUX

CAUSSES DE NIZAS
Carignan Vieilles Vignes 2002☆

2 hectares   6,000 bottles

John Goelet acquired this vineyard in 1998, adding to his collection of estates that includes the illustrious Clos du Val in California, Clover Mill in Tasmania, and Taltarni in Australia. This Carignan Vieilles Vignes 2002 has a dark purple tone and gives off flavours of toast and preserved fruit. It is firm and decisive on the palate. Overall, a well-structured wine.

John Goelet, SCEA Dom. Nizas et Salleles, Hameau de Salleles, 34720 Caux, tel. 04.67.90.17.92, fax 04.67.90.21.78, e-mail domnizas@wanadoo.fr
Tasting: by appt.

    € 11-15

CEVENNES

CLOS DE LA ROQUE
Pinot Noir 2001☆

1 hectare   4,000 bottles

This is Huguenot territory and the winery's sales office is housed in the former temple building. This Pinot Noir 2001 offers a sustained cherry colour and flavours of cherry and strawberry with a hint of liquorice. It is ample on the palate.

Yves et Anne-Marie Simon, 589, Le Ranquet, 30500 Saint-Ambroix, tel. 04.66.24.12.00, fax 04.66.24.12.00
Tasting: by appt.

   € 8-11

COLLINES DE LA MOURE

MAS DE MANTE
Vertige de la Moure 2001☆☆

1.5 hectares   7,000 bottles

The sixty-hectare Mas de Mante estate at the foot of La Gardiole Massif was acquired by the Lahoz and Boutennet families in 2001 and has since been given new life. This 2001 Syrah has an impeccable appearance and tastes of red-berries and liquorice. The estate's Domaine de Mujolan Blanc 2002 receives one star.

Dom. de Mujolan, Mas de Mante, RN 113, 34690 Fabrègues, tel. 04.67.85.11.06, fax 04.67.85.47.71,
e-mail contact@mujolan.com
Tasting: ev. day except Sun. 9am–12 noon 3pm–7pm

   € 11-15

DOMAINE SALVAT
Fenouil 2002☆☆
15 hectares   48,000 bottles

As of the 2003 vintage, Coteaux des Fenouillèdes wines will come under the Vin de Pays des Côtes Catalanes denomination. The jury acknowledged a Vin de Pays des Côtes Catalanes Fenouil Blanc 2002, but preferred this blend of Merlot, Syrah, and Grenache, with its bright purple sheen, flavours of red- and blackberries, its impressive silkiness on the palate and its persistently aromatic finish. A wine that is elegance personified.

Dom. Salvat, 8, av. Jean-Moulin, 66220 Saint-Paul-de-Fenouillet, tel. 04.68.59.29.00, fax 04.68.59.20.44, e-mail salvat.jp@wanadoo.fr
Tasting: by appt.

COTEAUX DU LIBRON

DOMAINE DE LA COLOMBETTE
Chardonnay Demi-muid Vinifié en Fût
de Chêne 2001☆☆

6.6 hectares

This Chardonnay 2001 – a Chardonnay in these parts? –
has green highlights. On the palate, it has a rare and subtle
elegance and is extremely aromatic, with hints of toasted
bread. The jury also acknowledged a most successful
Cabernet 2001.

François Pugibet, Dom. de la Colombette, anc. rte de Bédarieux,
34500 Béziers,
tel. 04.67.31.05.53, fax 04.67.30.46.65,
e-mail lacolombette@freesurf.fr
Tasting: by appt.

  € 8-11

DOMAINE DE PIERRE-BELLE
Réserve 2001☆☆☆ 🏆

0.9 hectares   5,600 bottles

This Réserve 2001 from Syrah grapes has the ruby-red colour
and touches of violet that constitute the very essence of the
Midi, the Pays d'Oc. Blackberries and blackcurrant aromas vie
with each other, with a hint of cocoa and a suggestion of wood
from cask maturation. A full, fleshy wine with tannins so silky
that one seems to be drinking pure velvet.

Michel Laguna, Dom. de Pierre-Belle, 34290 Lieuran-lès-Béziers,
tel. 04.67.36.15.58, fax 04.67.36.15.58,
e-mail pierrebelle@chez.com
Tasting: ev. day 9.30am–12 noon 3.30pm–7pm

   € 8-11

DOMAINE DE CIFFRE
Val Taurou 2001☆☆

3 hectares   12,000 bottles

This 2001 derives from a happy marriage of Cabernet Sauvignon (50%), Syrah, and a touch of Grenache grapes and is a signature wine from this domaine, acquired in 1998. The wine is a very dark red and its flavours arise from a pleasing blend of red-berries and roasted coffee, boosted by twelve months' cask maturation. On the palate, the wine is agreeably round and friendly, with a suggestion of butter, which takes nothing away from the underlying pungency of the fruit.

Lésineau, SARL Ch. Moulin de Ciffre, 34480 Autignac,
tel. 04.67.90.11.45, fax 04.67.90.12.05,
e-mail info@moulindeciffre.com
Tasting: by appt.

 € 8-11

DOMAINE DE COUJAN
Rolle 2002☆

5 hectares   26,600 bottles

Rolle is not exclusive to the AC Bellet. In this instance, it has resulted in a light and luminous straw-coloured wine with a nose that is redolent of a florist's shop. It is sprightly on the palate and should prove excellent with smoked salmon.

SCEA F. Guy et S. Peyre, Ch. Coujan, 34490 Murviel-lès-Béziers,
tel. 04.67.37.80.00, fax 04.67.37.86.23,
e-mail coujan@mnet.fr
Tasting: ev. day 9am–12 noon 2.30pm–7pm

 € 3-5

DOM. DE RAVANES
Les Gravières du Taurou Grande Réserve 2000☆☆
3.2 hectares   13,000 bottles

Equal parts of Merlot et Petit Verdot have gone into this unusual and strikingly coloured 2000 with its rich, lively hint of balsam, phenomenally empyreumatic – charred – nose, and its appealingly dense and solidly structured palate. The wine finishes on an aromatic note, with the silkiness of the Merlot balanced by the liveliness of the Petit Verdot.

Guy et Marc Benin, Dom. de Ravanès, 34490 Thézan-lès-Béziers, tel. 04.67.36.00.02, fax 04.67.36.35.64, e-mail ravanes@wanadoo.fr Tasting: by appt.

 € 15-23

COTES CATALANES

ARNAUD DE VILLENEUVE
Muscat Moelleux 2002☆
15 hectares   3,000 bottles

The cooperative cellars of Salses and Rivesaltes pooled resources ten years ago to represent 3,000 hectares planted with twenty or so different grape varieties. This Muscat 2002 is made predominantly (80%) from the Alexandria grape, with a small quantity of Muscat à Petits Grains added to yield a sweet wine with emerald tinges. The wine is distinctively fresh on the palate and the finish is refined and sustained. The hand is perhaps not iron, but the glove is decidedly velvet.

Les Vignobles du Rivesaltais, 1, rue de la Roussillonnaise, BP 56, 66600 Rivesaltes, tel. 04.68.64.06.63, fax 04.68.64.64.69, e-mail vignobles.rivesaltais@wanadoo.fr Tasting: by appt.

 € 3-5

DOMAINE BOUDAU
Le Petit Clos 2002☆
4 hectares   18,000 bottles

Brother and sister Pierre and Véronique Boudau took over
at the helm of this eighty-hectare family estate ten years
ago. Grenache, Syrah, and Cinsault grape varieties combine
in this forthright rosé, with its gooseberry colour shading
to a bouquet of violets and white peach. The Petit Clos 2002
is lively on the palate and has remarkable length for a rosé.
The estate's Muscat Sec 2002 was also awarded a star.

**Dom. Boudau, 6, rue Marceau, 66600 Rivesaltes,
tel. 04.68.64.45.37, fax 04.68.64.46.26,
e-mail domaineboudau@wanadoo.fr
Tasting: ev. day except Sun. 10am–12 noon 3pm–7pm;
cl. Sat. in winter**

  € 3-5

DOMAINE LAFAGE
Côté Est 2002☆
2.8 hectares   30,000 bottles

This family owned estate was taken over in 1995 and has since
been renovated. It draws largely on the experience of Jean-Marc
Lafarge, who previously worked as a wine-grower overseas.
This individualistic 2002 is a blend of Sauvignon (45%),
Chardonnay (30%), Grenache Blanc (20%), and Muscat (5%)
grape varieties. It is straw-coloured with green highlights and
has a nose redolent of fruit flavours, which persist on the palate.

**SCEA Dom. Lafage, Mas Durand, 66140 Canet-en-Roussillon,
tel. 04.68.80.35.82, fax 04.68.80.38.90,
e-mail domaine.lafage@wanadoo.fr
Tasting: by appt.**

     € 8-11

COTES DE PERIGNAN

J.-M. HORTALA
Les Coustades Elevé en Fût de Chêne 2000☆

1.5 hectares   6,000 bottles

This family owned estate goes back to 1893 and produces wines in the Languedoc tradition, including this Coustades 2000, with its attractive colour and its unusual mix of aromas, vacillating between musk and smoke. The wine is lively and decidedly interesting on the palate.

Jean-Marie Hortala, 20, rue Diderot, 11560 Fleury-d'Aude, tel. 04.68.33.37.74, fax 04.68.33.37.75, e-mail vins-hortala@wanadoo.fr
Tasting: by appt.

 € 8-11

CHATEAU DE LA NEGLY
Palazy 2002☆

1.5 hectares   7,500 bottles

This family château stands facing the sea in the massif of La Clape. The 2002 rosé has a clear salmon-pink colour and boasts a fresh and floral nose, finishing round and deliciously fruity. A wine to be drunk among friends, possibly to accompany a mixed grill.

Jean Paux-Rosset, SCEA Ch. de la Négly, 11560 Fleury-d'Aude, tel. 04.68.32.36.28, fax 04.68.32.10.69, e-mail lanegly@wanadoo.fr
Tasting: by appt.

 € 3-5

HUGUES DE BEAUVIGNAC
Sauvignon 2002☆

40 hectares   150,000 bottles

A top-of-the-range Sauvignon 2002 from this cooperative.
A very light-coloured appearance is backed up by a range of
elegant flavours of citrus fruits and white flowers. The wine
leaves a highly commendable freshness on the palate. The
cooperative's Rosé de Syrah 2002 is also awarded a star.

**Cave les Costières de Pomérols, 34810 Pomérols,
tel. 04.67.77.01.59, fax 04.67.77.77.21
Tasting: by appt.**

     € 3-5

DOMAINE DE MARIE-ANAIS
Syrano 2001☆

1.1 hectares   6,900 bottles

The cellars of this family owned domaine are housed in a
converted barn and the domaine itself takes its name from
that of the family's only daughter. Merlot and Syrah grapes
are assembled into an attractive dark purple wine with a
distinctive and persistent nose of red-berries and a well-
structured and comparatively rounded palate.

**André Garcia, Dom. de Marie-Anaïs,
16, rue Basassac, 34510 Florensac,
tel. 04.67.77.04.18, fax 04.67.77.04.18
Tasting: by appt.**

     € 5-8

COTES DE THONGUE

DOMAINE DE L'ARJOLLE
Merlot Synthèse 2001☆

8 hectares   70,000 bottles

"Synthesis" is an apt choice of name for this Merlot 2001 from the Domaine de l'Arjolle. The wine is garnet red with a hint of brick; the nose slightly vanilla-flavoured, and the palate aromatic and full-bodied. A well-balanced wine. The Arjolle Sauvignon 2002 is also awarded a star.

Dom. de L'Arjolle, 6, rue de la Côte, 34480 Pouzolles, tel. 04.67.24.81.18, fax 04.67.24.81.90, e-mail domaine@arjolle.com
Tasting: ev. day except Sun. 8am–12 noon 2pm–6pm

  € 11-15

DOMAINE DE LA CROIX BELLE
Cascaïllou 2001☆☆

1.07 hectares   4,000 bottles

Made predominantly from Grenache Noir grapes with added Syrah and Mourvèdre, this 2001 boasts a pronounced colour and a nose that is nuanced, with a hint of fruit. An elegant and well-structured blend that might best accompany a veal roast.

Jacques et Françoise Boyer, Dom. La Croix-Belle, 34480 Puissalicon, tel. 04.67.36.27.23, fax 04.67.36.60.45, e-mail information@croix.belle.com
Tasting: ev. day 8am–12 noon 2pm–6pm; Sun. by appt.

    € 11-15

MONTARELS
Sauvignon 2002☆
60 hectares   60,000 bottles

Vins de pays have the singular and appealing merit of
refreshing our knowledge of geography. Côtes de Thongue?
Where exactly is that? In any event, this clear and lustrous
Sauvignon 2002 simply explodes with fruit flavours and
proves to be an excellent ambassador for the area. The aromas
are well-defined and the wine has a vivacity that earmarks
it as an excellent aperitif, possibly even with crème de cassis
or a dash of blackberry liqueur. The jury also singled out
a Vent des Collines rouge 2001 as being most accomplished.

**Cave Co-op. Alignan-du-Vent, rue Lissac, 34290 Alignan-du-Vent,
tel. 04.67.24.91.31, fax 04.67.24.96.22,
e-mail info@cavecooperative.com
Tasting: ev. day except Sat. Sun. 8am–12 noon 1.30pm–5.30pm**

DOMAINE DE MONT D'HORTES
Sauvignon 2002☆☆☆ 🏆
2.2 hectares   16,000 bottles

Some *vins de pays* are fit to be up there with the best wines,
as witness this Sauvignon 2002 from a domaine along the Via
Domitia, where a Roman villa once stood. A brilliantly clear
golden straw colour and a nose that takes off like a rocket; but for
all its dynamism, it retains its dignity and intense fruit flavours.
Equal vivacity persists on the palate, where the wine emerges
as pungent and full-bodied, impressively full of flavour.

**Jacques Anglade et Fils, Dom. de Mont d'Hortes, 34630 Saint-Thibéry,
tel. 04.67.77.88.08, fax 04.67.30.17.57
Tasting: ev. day 9am–12 noon 2pm–6pm**

DOMAINE MONTPLEZY
Félicité 2001☆☆
0.42 hectares   1,700 bottles

This 2001 from the Domaine Montplézy near Pézenas is felicitous indeed: a blend where the Carignan grape variety predominates, with the addition of some Grenache. The appearance is distinguished less by its colour than by its luminosity. The gentle finesse of the bouquet carries over onto the palate, where it is difficult to conceive of a more subtle sensation. A rack of lamb with rosemary would undoubtedly bring out the best in this aptly named Félicité 2001.

Anne Sutra de Germa et Christian Gil, Dom. Montplézy, 34120 Pézenas, tel. 04.67.98.27.81, fax 04.67.98.27.81, e-mail domainemontplezy@free.fr
Tasting: by appt.

 € 11-15

TARRAL
Sauvignon 2002☆
11.57 hectares   45,000 bottles

Tarral came into being following the 1995 merger of the cooperative cellars of Valros and Pouzolles in the windswept area known as the Côtes de Thongue. This clear golden Sauvignon 2002 has a nose full of fruit and an elegant structure lifted by the merest hint of sparkle. A wine ideally suited to accompany prawns, oysters au gratin, or mussels in a white Sauvignon sauce.

UCA le Tarral, Site de Valros, av. de la Montagne, 34290 Valros, tel. 04.67.98.52.65, fax 04.67.98.59.54, e-mail info@tarral.com
Tasting: ev. day except Sat. Sun. 9am–12 noon 2pm–4pm

     € 3-5

MAS DE FORTON 2001 ☆☆

30 hectares   100,000 bottles

The Durand family specializes in the production of "Roman" wines, marketing the celebrated Orpailleur label from Quebec and, not least, making *vins de pays* like this blend of Syrah and Merlot grapes. The 2001 is a luminous ruby red, with a nose that carries pronounced aromas of cherry and raspberry. Its tannins have already softened to produce a wine that is delicate yet well-balanced on the palate.

Hervé et Guilhem Durand, 4294, rte de Bellegarde, 30300 Beaucaire, tel. 04.66.59.19.72, fax 04.66.59.50.80, e-mail contact@tourelles.com
Tasting: by appt.

 € 3-5

LEYRIS MAZIERE 2001 ☆☆

12 hectares 1,500 bottles

This tiny property, amounting to just over one tenth of a hectare, produces an interesting blend of Carignan (30%) and Alicante grape varieties. The 2001 in question is dark violet in colour, with a nose that is redolent of the nearby garrigue scrubland, together with balsamic undertones. On the palate it develops a distinctly velvet feel.

Leyris Mazière, chem. des Pouges, 30260 Cannes-et-Clairan, tel. 04.66.93.05.98, fax 04.66.93.05.98, e-mail gilles.leyris@libertysurf.fr
Tasting: by appt.

 € 15-23

DOMAINE DE MOLINES
Vieilles Vignes 2000☆
4 hectares   40,000 bottles

Four hectares of this 100-hectare domaine are given over to Cabernet Sauvignon vines. This Vieilles Vignes 2000 is intensely dark in colour, with a nose rich in spices and red-berries. It opens cleanly and develops quite generously on the palate.

EARL Roger Gassier, Ch. de Nages, 30132 Caissargues,
tel. 04.66.38.44.30, fax 04.66.38.44.21,
e-mail i.roquelaure@michelgassier.com
Tasting: by appt.

     € 5-8

HERAULT

MAS DE DAUMAS GASSAC 2002☆☆
12 hectares

Tiny patches of vines are dotted around clearings in this vast forest, for all the world like an enchanted wood in a fairytale. It is a matter of historical record that the monk St Benoît d'Aniane declared his preference for Languedoc over his native Burgundy and settled here to work this land. Viognier, Chardonnay, Petit Manseng, and thirty other grape varieties in minuscule quantities go into this golden 2002, whose bouquet recalls that of white flowers with a hint of vanilla. A wine that is fresh and balanced on the palate. Equally remarkable is the Mas de Daumas Gassac Rouge 2001.

Famille Guibert, SAS Moulin de Gassac, Mas de Daumas Gassac,
34150 Aniane,
tel. 04.67.57.71.28, fax 04.67.57.41.03,
e-mail contact@daumas-gassac.com
Tasting: ev. day 10am–12.30pm 2pm–6.30pm; groups by appt.

   € 30-38

DOMAINE DE JONQUIERES 2001 ☆

2 hectares   6,000 bottles

Wines from Jonquières have been exported since as far back as 1870, notably to Canada. The dry 2001 white from this historic family owned château draws on grape varieties planted on a limestone gravel soil: Chenin (40%), Grenache Blanc (45%), Roussanne, and Viognier. The wine has a clear straw colour, while the nose suggests nine months of in-cask maturation in addition to floral overtones. The palate has body and roundness – a highly successful vintage.

François de Cabissole, Ch. de Jonquières, 34725 Jonquières,
tel. 04.67.96.62.58, fax 04.67.88.61.92,
e-mail chateau.de.jonquieres@wanadoo.fr
Tasting: by appt.

  € 11-15

DOMAINE JORDY
Marselan 2001 ☆☆

1 hectare

This Marselan 2001, grown on a tiny corner of the domaine, is a blend of Cabernet Sauvignon and Grenache Noir grape varieties. The colour is dark and intense; the subsequent flavours evoke blackberry and blackcurrant with an acceptable hint of wood. Overall, a silky-bodied wine that deserves to be drunk in the company of one's best friends.

Frédéric Jordy, Loiras, 9, rte de Salelles, 34700 Le Bosc,
tel. 04.67.44.70.30, fax 04.67.44.76.54
Tasting: ev. day except Sun. 8am–8pm

   € 15-23

MAS DE JANINY
Cabernet Sauvignon 2001☆☆
1.8 hectares   5,000 bottles

A bottle that one might purchase for no other reason than on account of its most attractive label. That said, the contents of this 2001 are on a par with its aesthetic presentation: intensely deep red in colour, it develops a strong personality building on pungent aromas of undergrowth and ripe fruit. The body exhibits good and unctuous tannins and the long finish is a bouquet of aromas.

**Julien Frères, Mas de Janiny, 21, pl. de la Pradette,
34230 Saint-Bazille-de-la-Sylve,
tel. 04.67.57.96.70, fax 04.67.57.96.77,
e-mail julien-thierry@wanadoo.fr
Tasting: by appt.**

 € 5-8

DOMAINE DE MOULINES
Merlot 2002☆
20 hectares   210,000 bottles

There were twenty-eight hectares under cultivation when the domaine was acquired in 1914. There are 55 hectares today – a tribute to the work of three generations. This Merlot 2002 has good, sustained colour and elegant and complex aromas of overripe fruit. It is well-structured and agreeably full-bodied. A wine that is faithful to its heritage. The Cuvée Prestige 2001 is also awarded one star.

**Michel Saumade, GFA Mas de Moulines, 34130 Mudaison,
tel. 04.67.70.20.48, fax 04.67.87.50.05
Tasting: ev. day except Sun. 9am–12 noon 2pm–7pm**

 € 3-5

DOMAINE LES QUATRE PILAS
Cuvée de la Mouchère 2001☆☆☆ 🏆

1.3 hectares   5,000 bottles

Cleared garrigue scrubland makes a positive contribution to this harmonious blend of Cabernet Franc, Cabernet Sauvignon, and Marselan grape varieties. The tone of this 2001 is a very dark red. Mint-flavour notes form a counterpoint to strong aromas of blackcurrant. The wine has body and texture, combining in perfect harmony yet retaining its individuality. By any standards, an exceptional wine.

Joseph Bousquet, chem. de Pignan, 34570 Murviel-lès-Montpellier, tel. 04.67.47.89.32, fax 04.67.47.89.32
Tasting: by appt.

   € 8-11

MONTS DE LA GRAGE

DOMAINE DES SOULIE
Merlot 2000☆☆

2 hectares   5,000 bottles

The Domaine des Soulié has been in the same family for many, many years. Today, it occupies thirty hectares of organically cultivated vines. This garnet red Merlot 2000 has distinctive amber highlights, which attest to fifteen months of in-cask maturation. Full-bodied and warm fruit flavours delight the palate. A wine that is ready to be drunk as of now.

Aurore et Rémy Soulié, Dom. des Soulié, Carriera de la Teuliera, 34360 Assignan,
tel. 04.67.38.11.78, fax 04.67.38.19.31, e-mail remy.soulie@wanadoo.fr
Tasting: by appt.

     € 3-5

OC

DOMAINE D'AIGUES BELLES
Cuvée Lombarde 2001☆

1.85 hectares   5,884 bottles

Bon coq gaulois ne boit que vin (a real Frenchman drinks only wine) was the dogmatic slogan once appended to this domaine, established in 1870 by Eugène Bosc. Some years ago, the twenty-hectare estate was revamped and replanted with a selection of noble grape varieties, best-illustrated perhaps by this Cuvée Lombarde 2001, a mix of Grenache, Merlot, and Cabernet. The wine shows early signs of ageing well. It has traces of vanilla and of floral notes from the Grenache. The 2001 opens amiably, with tannins becoming more pronounced.

Nicole Palatan, Dom. d'Aigues Belles, 30260 Brouzet-les-Quissac, tel. 06.07.48.74.65, fax 01.46.43.86.96
Tasting: by appt.

 € 8-11

DOMAINE DE BAUBIAC
Merlot 2001☆

1.37 hectares   9,000 bottles

Voltaire once suggested that "to win is not enough, it is essential to seduce". This frank Merlot 2001 would appear to heed his admonition to the letter. The wine is a distinctive garnet red, the nose a complex amalgam of very ripe fruit and charred wood, the palate rich in well-established tannins. A wine with winning and seductive ways.

SCEA Dom. de Baubiac, 29, av. du 11-Novembre, 30260 Quissac, tel. 04.66.77.33.45, fax 04.66.77.33.45, e-mail philip@dstu.univ-montp2.fr
Tasting: by appt.

 € 5-8

DOMAINE DE LA BAUME 2000☆

1.97 hectares   2,500 bottles

This 2000 is a Cabernet Sauvignon through and through, with a colour that hints at red brick, a maturing nose with aromas of pepper, and a long finish that is full and robust with a suggestion of wood.

Dom. de la Baume, rte de Pézenas, RN 9, 34290 Servian, tel. 04.67.39.29.49, fax 04.67.39.29.40
Tasting: by appt.

  € 15-23

DOMAINE DE BEAUSEJOUR JUDELL
Impatience Cabernet-Merlot 2001☆

3.6 hectares   20,000 bottles

Adelaide-born Australian Graeme Judell and his French wife Catherine fell in love with this domaine in 1998 and decided to settle here and restore it to its former glory. Their "impatience" to do so, reflected in the name of this 2001 red, is readily understood. The wine itself, a 50:50 mix of Merlot and Cabernet Sauvignon grapes, is a clear ruby red with an expressive bouquet that suggests vegetal matter. It is a robust wine with modulated tannins, and can be laid down with confidence until being brought out and served with game.

Graeme Judell, TM 14, RN 9, 34800 Nébian, tel. 04.67.96.27.80, fax 04.67.96.39.57, e-mail contact@beausejour-judell.com
Tasting: ev. day except Sat. Sun. 9am–6pm

   € 8-11

DOMAINE DE LA BERGERIE D'AMILHAC
Syrah 2001☆☆
1.2 hectares   10,000 bottles

Never let it be said that the winemakers of Chablis have no taste for adventure. Christian Adine is a case in point, one of numerous Burgundian winemakers who have upped stakes and come to work in the Midi. He opted to settle on this twenty-hectare estate with a characteristic *mas* at its hub, wild boar, and partridges on his doorstep, and Syrah and Chardonnay vines all around. His Syrah 2001 is as purple as it gets, with violet highlights and aromas of wild strawberries all the way through to a glorious finish. It could be said that his Cabernet Sauvignon 2001 might also tempt the pillars of the Chablis establishment to drop by for dinner when they are in the vicinity.

EARL Christian Adine, 2, allée du Château, 89800 Courgis, tel. 03.86.41.40.28, fax 03.86.41.45.75, e-mail nicole.adine@free.fr

    € 3-5

LE BOSC
Syrah 2002☆☆
7 hectares   50,000 bottles

Warm, luminous, aromatic – a typical pays d'Oc Syrah with all the vitality of a flamenco dancer. This Syrah 2000 is a delight on the palate – deep, languid, and sustained. A treat with small game.

**SICA Delta Domaines, Dom. du Bòsc, 34450 Vias, tel. 04.67.21.73.54, fax 04.67.21.68.38
Tasting: by appt.**

 € 3-5

DOMAINE LE BOUIS

Zoé 2001☆

6 hectares   12,000 bottles

This vintage is dedicated to the owners' eldest daughter, Zoé. Made from 100% Carignan, this 2001 exhibits a deep-purple colour with even brighter purple highlights. Aromas of spices and red-berries gradually develop and become increasingly pronounced. This spiciness is again apparent on the palate, adding up to a wine that is supple and eminently drinkable.

De Keroualtz, SCEA CH. Le Bouïs, rte Bleue, 11430 Gruissan, tel. 04.68.75.25.25, fax 04.68.75.25.26, e-mail chateau-le-bouis@wanadoo.fr
Tasting: by appt.

 € 5-8

CALVET DE CALVET

Chardonnay 2002☆

65,000 bottles

Calvet de Calvet: almost the name of a chic perfume, but in this case it's a Chardonnay 2002 – a blend of Cabernet Sauvignon, Merlot, and Syrah grape varieties with a beautiful golden colour and a nose redolent of honeysuckle. On the palate, this 2002 achieves a pleasing roundness by sacrificing a certain vivacity, which in no way detracts from the overall harmony.

Calvet, 75, cours du Médoc, BP 11, 33028 Bordeaux Cedex, tel. 05.56.43.59.00, fax 05.56.43.17.78, e-mail calvet@calvet.com

 € 3-5

CAMAS
Pinot Noir 2001☆
20 hectares   15,000 bottles

An attractively luminous cherry-red Pinot Noir that succeeds in far-from-easy conditions a long way from home. This 2001 makes the grade, however, subtly making the most of its black-fruit flavours. Good with chicken – of the free range variety.

Cave Anne de Joyeuse, 41, av. Charles-de-Gaulle, 11300 Limoux, tel. 04.68.74.79.40, fax 04.68.74.79.49, e-mail fabre.adj@wanadoo.fr Tasting: by appt.

    € 5-8

DOMAINE CAMP-GALHAN
Liqueyrol 2001☆
4 hectares   10,300 bottles

Alain and Lionel Pourquier exemplify a phenomenon observed quite frequently of late: in 2000, they left the bosom of the cooperative to grow and commercialize their own output. This go-it-alone decision was underpinned by their acquisition of the Camp Galhan domaine, a terroir comprised of rolled shingle deposits left by the Gardon. Merlot and Cabernet Sauvignon have been combined to impart a deep colour to this Liqueyrol 2001, with its hints of toasted bread complementing aromas of gooseberry and raspberry. The palate still has a suggestion of wood, resulting from twelve months' cask maturation, but the overall effect remains unimpaired and balanced.

GAEC de la Roque, 1, rue des Aires, 30720 Ribautes-Les-Tavernes, tel. 04.66.83.48.47, fax 04.66.83.56.92, e-mail colioaires@worldonline.fr Tasting: Mon. Wed. Fri. 2pm–6.30pm; Sat. 9.30am–12 noon 2pm–6.30pm

   € 11-15

DOMAINE DE CHAMBERT
Chardonnay 2002☆

100,000 bottles

Chardonnay would appear to be as much at home in the Pays d'Oc as it seems to be anywhere else in the world. This straw-yellow 2002 has the now-familiar bouquet of acacia and hawthorn blossom, but opens unusually pleasantly on the palate and sustains well. It is also moderately priced – which, as they say, never hurts.

SA Chantovent, Quai du Port-au-Vin, BP 7, 78270 Bonnières-sur-Seine, tel. 01.30.98.59.01, fax 01.30.98.59.19, e-mail adv.france@chantovent.com

DOMAINE LES CHARMETTES
La Magdelaine 2001☆

2 hectares   5,000 bottles

Viognier, Grenache Blanc, Sauvignon, Terret, Chardonnay: the list goes on and on in the case of this Magdelaine 2001. Pale gold in colour and with familiar aromas of hawthorn and acacia blossom, it goes on to develop strong flavours of lemon and grapefruit. A pleasurable wine produced at Les Carmettes, a property acquired in 1987 by a family that already operates another forty-hectare domaine.

Famille Alcon, Dom. Les Charmettes, Rte de Florensac, 34340 Marseillan, tel. 04.67.77.66.16, fax 04.67.77.66.16, e-mail alcon.nicolas@laposte.net Tasting: by appt.

DOMAINE DU CHATEAU D'EAU
Cabernet Sauvignon 2001☆

4.5 hectares   40,000 bottles

From the aptly named Domaine du Château d'Eau, whose
square tower overlooks the sea, the Montagnes Noires and
(on occasion even) the Pyrénées, comes this Cabernet
Sauvignon 2001 that also occupies a dominant position.
Blood-red in colour and with pronounced aromas of very
ripe red-berries and peppers, this 2001 persists on the palate,
combining distinctive flavours with non-obtrusive tannins.
The producer? None other than Moillard from Nuits-Saint-
Georges, one of numerous vintners attracted to the Languedoc
region, where Moillard now operates a far-from-modest
eighty-four hectare estate.

Dom. du Château d'Eau, c/o B. Montariol, 34290 Lieuran-Les-Béziers,
tel. 03.80.62.42.22, e-mail nuicave@wanadoo.fr
Prop: Moillard

 € 3-5

CIGALUS 2000☆

15 hectares   26,000 bottles

Gérard Bertrand, who already owns, among others, the
Domaine Villemajou in Corbières and the Château Hospitalet
at La Clape, acquired this property in 1997. In the main, this
2000 combines Merlot and Cabernet Sauvignon grapes to offer
a wine with red-tile highlights and complex aromas of leather
and cherry brandy. A full-bodied wine with discreet wood
notes and a good finish.

Gérard Bertrand, Ch. Hospitalet, rte de Narbonne-Plage, 11100 Narbonne,
tel. 04.68.45.36.00, fax 04.68.45.27.17,
e-mail vins@gerard-bertrand.com
Tasting: by appt.

 € 23-30

DOMAINE DE LA CLAPIERE
Jalade 2002☆
0.84 hectares   4,300 bottles

This manor house dates back to the seventeenth century
and was built by one François Clapier, who left France shortly
after the repeal of the Edict of Nantes. The local population
commonly referred to the manor as "La Clapière" and the
name has stuck until today. The Jalade 2000 is a delightful
and discreetly coloured rosé, unequivocally fresh and fruity
from first to last. This is an extraordinarily vivacious wine
that, above all, bears witness to the successful textural
marriage between the Cinsault and Syrah grape varieties.

Dom. de la Clapière, 34530 Montagnac,
tel. 04.67.34.07.52, fax 04.67.24.06.16,
e-mail laclapierewines@wanadoo.fr
Tasting: by appt.

 € 5-8

CLOS DEL REY
Grenache-Carignan 2001☆
10 hectares   5,000 bottles

After twenty-six years spent working in a cooperative wine
cellar, Jacques Montagné elected to take matters into his
own hands. His twenty-hectare Clos nestles in the shadow
of the Château de Queribus in the heart of garrigue scrubland.
Carignan and Grenache grape varieties are teamed in this
instance to yield a deep garnet wine with a residual hint
of wood from twelve months of in-cask maturation. This
Grenache-Carignan 2001 is a complex wine with unobtrusive
tannins. It has already reached maturity.

Jacques Montagné, 7, rue Barbusse, 66460 Maury,
tel. 04.68.59.15.08, fax 04.68.59.15.08

 € 23-30

CONDAMINE BERTRAND
Petit Verdot Gourmandise 2001☆☆
1 hectare   6,000 bottles

This Petit Verdot from a splendid eighteenth century château domaine has not only a magnificent cardinal's robe of a colour, but all the other hallmarks of a great wine. Its mint bouquet is as delightful as its elegant structure and the quality of its tannins are admirable. A perfect accompaniment perhaps to braised beef – albeit not quite yet: this 2001 is still improving and will benefit from being laid down for some years.

B. Jany, Ch. Condamine Bertrand, RN 9, 34230 Paulhan,
tel. 04.67.25.27.96, fax 04.67.25.07.55,
e-mail chateau.condamineber@wanadoo.fr
Tasting: ev. day except Sun. 10am–12 noon 2pm–6pm

   € 23-30

LA CROIX DU PIN
Cinsault Cuvée Prestige 2002☆
8 hectares   70,000 bottles

A very moderately priced Cinsault rosé that has the added attraction of being, quite simply, a good wine. The colour is salmon-pink, the nose is lively, and the wine performs well on the palate. An "easy-drinking" rosé in the best sense of the term.

La Fiée des Lois, 21, rue Montgolfier, BP 90022,
79232 Prahecq Cedex,
tel. 05.49.32.15.15, fax 05.49.32.16.05,
e-mail selection@fdlois.fr

    € -3

GEORGES DUBOEUF
Merlot Cuvée Prestige 2001☆
60,000 bottles

Georges Duboeuf may well rule the roost in Beaujolais, but
he is also to be found elsewhere – in Poitou, for example,
and here in the Languedoc. His Merlot Prestige 2001
is rosy-cheeked and fresh-complexioned, with overripe fruit
predominating. The palate is silky, rounded, and full-bodied.
Duboeuf has emerged as an important négociant intermediary
between wine-growers and the marketplace.

**SA Les Vins Georges Duboeuf, La Gare, BP 12,
71570 Romanèche-Thorins,
tel. 03.85.35.34.20, fax 03.85.35.34.25,
e-mail gduboeuf@duboeuf.com
Tasting: ev. day 9am–6pm at Hameau-en-Beaujolais;
cl. New Year's Day–15 Jan**

 €3-5

DOMAINE ELLUL-FERRIERES
Vieilles Vignes 2000☆
5,000 bottles

A "boutique winery", as they say in California: a three-
hectare property planted with Grenache acquired in 1997
that has been expanded into a small (seven-hectare) domaine.
This Vieilles Vignes 2000 has a pleasing colour with brick-red
highlights commensurate with its age. The nose and palate
are promisingly fruity and sustained. A supple wine available
only in a limited quantity, so it's best to order now.

**Dom. Ellul-Ferrières, Fontmagne, RN 110, 34160 Castries,
tel. 06.15.38.45.01, fax 04.67.16.04.49,
e-mail ellulferrieres@aol.com
Tasting: ev. day 5pm–7pm**

 €8-11

LOUIS FABRE
Chardonnay 2002☆
10 hectares   80,000 bottles

The shadow of the Viscount de la Courtade, a vassal in the service of the Bishop of Béziers, hangs over the sixteenth century manor house surrounded by this seventy-hectare domaine, which has produced a Chardonnay 2002 with an impeccable colour. Classic aromas of acacia and hawthorn blossom on the nose, and a palate that has body and character. Excellent with fish prepared in a sauce.

Louis Fabre, rue du Château, 11200 Luc-sur-Orbieu,
tel. 04.68.27.10.80, fax 04.68.27.38.19,
e-mail chateauluc@aol.com
Tasting: by appt.

  € 3-5

DOMAINE DE LA FADEZE
Merlot Elevé en Fût de Chêne 2000☆☆
4 hectares   15,000 bottles

The 2000 is a pure Merlot whose body already shows early indications of ageing. The bouquet has a certain *élan,* with wood notes complemented by aromas of fruit. The wine is quite well-structured with unobtrusive tannins.

Lenthéric, Dom. La Fadèze, 34340 Marseillan,
tel. 04.67.77.26.42, fax 04.67.77.20.92
Tasting: ev. day except Sun. 9am–12 noon 2pm–6pm

 € 8-11

DOMAINE FAURE
Cinsault 2002☆
0.29 hectares   1,734 bottles

A peach-coloured Cinsault rosé that is made to measure from a domaine that extends a warm welcome to visitors and artists alike. The wine boasts delicately balanced aromas of flowers and fruit. It opens perhaps over-modestly but finishes honourably. The domaine's Merlot 2002 also receives a star.

Denis Faure, 1, av. de la Liberté, 11300 La Digne-d'Aval, tel. 04.68.31.72.66, fax 04.68.31.72.66
Tasting: by appt.

    € 3-5

DOMAINE DE LA FERRANDIERE
Grenache Gris 2002☆
6 hectares   60,000 bottles

Jacques Gau and his co-workers currently cultivate some seventy hectares of vines together with twenty-five-hectares of apple trees. The domaine is situated at Aigues-Vives, where the salt air represents a clear disadvantage, but Gau and his team are fighting back, as witness this Grenache Gris 2002 with its lustrous peach-blossom colour and its sprightly flavours on the palate, which are not without a certain elegance. A refined wine, suited perhaps to an exotic cuisine.

SARL Les Ferrandières, Dom. de La Ferrandière, 11800 Aigues-Vives, tel. 04.68.79.29.30, fax 04.68.79.29.39,
e-mail info@ferrandiere.com
Tasting: ev. day except Sat. Sun. 8am–12 noon 2pm–6pm
Prop: Jacques Gau

    € 3-5

DOMAINE FONT-MARS
Mourvèdre-Syrah 2001☆

3.8 hectares   15,000 bottles

Wine has been produced on this Gallo-Roman domaine since 1878. Dark-red; ripe fruit and dried nuts; handsome and harmonious structure and tannin. Good with soft cheese.

GFA Font-Mars, rte de Marseillan, 34140 Mèze,
tel. 04.67.43.81.19, fax 04.67.43.79.41, e-mail info@font-mars.com
Tasting: by appt. Prop: Jean-Baptiste de Clock

 € 8-11

GRANGE DES ROUQUETTE
Agrippa 2001☆☆

2 hectares   6,000 bottles

Imperial purple, with a bouquet of pungent fruit and spices. In all, a genuinely rounded wine.

Vignobles Boudinaud, Grand-Rue, 30210 Fournes,
tel. 04.66.37.27.23, fax 04.66.37.03.56,
e-mail boudinaud@infonie.fr
Tasting: by appt.

 € 5-8

DOMAINE LAMARGUE
Syrah 2001☆

2.5 hectares   13,000 bottles

Ruby colour with dark purple highlights; rich in fruit aromas; supple and persistent. Ninty per cent of production is exported.

Ch. Lamargue, rte de Vauvert, 30800 Saint-Gilles,
tel. 04.66.87.31.89, e-mail domaine-de-lamargue@wanadoo.fr
Tasting: by appt.

 € 5-8

DOMAINE LAUGE
Cuvée Saint-Joly 2002☆

1.3 hectares

A 50:50 blend of Syrah and Carignan grape varieties underpins this well-made and individualistic wine, with its body of deep garnet velvet. The nose detects aromas of musk and the wine opens in determined fashion with, so to speak, a double helping of flavours. Its finish is long and straightforward, with an unmistakable suggestion of liquorice.

GAEC Les Carretals, rue du Minervois, 34210 Aigne,
tel. 06.79.70.71.53, fax 04.68.91.13.42
Tasting: by appt.

   € 5-8

DOMAINE DES LAURIERS
Syrah-Grenache 2001☆☆

2 hectares   5,000 bottles

The domaine was established in 1969 (although the cellars date back to 1900) and has gradually expanded to its present forty-two-hectare surface area. The blackcurrant tinge that marks the tone of this Syrah-Grenache 2001 is echoed subsequently on the palate, together with floral and mineral notes. The wine is supple, balanced, and amply rounded.

Marc Chabrol, Dom. des Lauriers, 15, rte de Pézenas,
34120 Castelnau-de-Guers,
tel. 04.67.98.18.20, fax 04.67.98.96.49,
e-mail cabrol.marc@wanadoo.fr
Tasting: by appt.

 € 3-5

DOMAINE DE MAIRAN
Chardonnay Les Hauts de Mairan 2001☆☆

The eponymous Monsieur de Mairan was a dedicated physicist ennobled by Louis XV in recognition of his contributions to science. This time around, the honour goes to a gold-green Chardonnay 2001 which exudes discreet mineral aromas, notably flint. On the palate, the wine achieves a balance between strength and subtlety. From the same domaine come a most accomplished Cabernet Franc 2002 and a remarkable Cabernet Sauvignon 1999.

Jean Peitavy, Dom. de Mairan, 34620 Puisserguier,
tel. 04.67.93.74.20, fax 04.67.93.83.05
Tasting: ev. day 8am–8pm

 € 5-8

DOMAINE DE MALAVIEILLE
Charmille 2002☆
2.2 hectares   4,900 bottles

The soil of Salagou still carries the footprints of the dinosaurs, but it is now given over to Sauvignon, Viognier, and Chardonnay. These grape varieties impart to this Charmille 2002 its radiant, albeit somewhat pale colour, its delicately fresh floral aromas, and its flavours on the palate, which are lively and expressive, if rather short on the finish.

Mireille Bertrand, Malavieille, 34800 Mérifons,
tel. 04.67.96.34.67, fax 04.67.96.32.21
Tasting: by appt.

 € 5-8

DOMAINE DE MALLEMORT
Cuvée Alexandre 2000☆☆
1 hectare   3,600 bottles

Back in the Middle Ages, Mallemort was certainly not a place to be: it was here that capital punishment was meted out and the streets were typically festooned with bodies suspended from the hangman's noose. Times have changed, however, and there is today no reason to miss out on an *in situ* opportunity to taste this ruby-red Cuvée Alexandre 2000, a marriage of Cabernet Sauvignon (65%) and Merlot grapes that has been matured for twelve months in the vat and a further year in cask. The wine gives off intense aromas of preserved fruit underpinned by delicate spices, yielding to a silky finish devoid of harsh tannins.

**Luc Peitavy, Dom. de Mallemort, 34620 Puisserguier,
tel. 04.67.93.74.20, fax 04.67.93.83.05
Tasting: by appt.**

MAS MONTEL
Jéricho 2001☆☆
3 hectares   20,000 bottles

The Jericho 2001 is the offspring of a marriage of the Syrah (80%) and Grenache varieties. The wine boasts a colour of imperial purple, with aromas of musk and spices, and flavours heightened by excellent tannins. A compact, elegantly textured, and well-structured wine that would go well with sauces or dishes that include juniper berries.

**EARL Granier, Mas Montel, 30250 Aspères,
tel. 04.66.80.01.21, fax 04.66.80.01.87,
e-mail montel@wanadoo.fr
Tasting: ev. day except Sun. 9am–7pm**

DOMAINE DE MONTLOBRE
Tête de Cuvée 2000☆☆
20 hectares   6,000 bottles

The two domaines La Jasse and Montlobre were acquired a couple of years ago by a négociant from The Netherlands. Accordingly, this Tête de Cuvée 2000 from the latter estate might fly a Dutch flag, but its *lingua franca* is decidedly that of the Midi. The wine is a blend of Merlot and Cabernet, with a touch of Syrah for good measure. Its colour is deepest red with amber highlights and its bouquet attests to a long period of in-cask maturation, which has not, however, deprived the wine of its musky aroma. Well-proportioned tannins are such that this wine can be cellared for a further one or two years. The domaine's L'Ermitage Domaine des Deux Soleils Tête de Cuvée 2000 proved equally remarkable in the eyes of the tasting panel.

**SCEA Mas de La Jasse, La Jasse, 34980 Combaillaux,
tel. 04.67.67.04.04, fax 04.67.67.92.20,
e-mail f.quermel@jasse.fr
Tasting: by appt. Prop: Walraven**

 € 15-23

CELLIERS DES NEUF FIEFS
Sauvignon 2002☆☆
30,000 bottles

An accomplished golden Sauvignon that is clearly earmarked as an accompaniment to a seafood platter. The nose is rich and redolent of floral and plant notes, and this 2002 is lively, balanced and undeniably elegant.

**Les Coteaux de Neffiès, av. de la Gare, 34320 Neffiès,
tel. 04.67.24.61.98, fax 04.67.24.62.12,
e-mail cavecoop.neffies@wanadoo.fr
Tasting: by appt.**

 € 3-5

DOMAINE DE L'ORVIEL
Sauvignon 2002☆

1.5 hectares   6,400 bottles

This Sauvignon 2000 is the first wine to emerge from
a privately owned cellar that was entirely renovated when
the Cabane brothers left the cooperative. Judging by this
wine, the brothers are off to a good start: a sun-drenched
colour gives way to a cocktail of mildly exotic floral and
citrus aromas, followed by aromatic flavours that persist
on the palate through to a long and balanced finish.

**SCEA Cabane frères, Mas Flavard, 30350 Saint-Jean-de-Serres,
tel. 04.66.83.45.96, fax 04.66.83.45.96
Tasting: by appt.**

 € 5-8

DOMAINE PREIGNES LE VIEUX
Cuvée Preixanum 2002☆

4.5 hectares   10,000 bottles

This domaine is situated on agricultural land going back
a thousand years. The Vic family – the current proprietors –
will celebrate their century as owners in 2005. Viognier and
Vermentino grapes share the honours in this Cuvée Preixanum
2002. The body is golden with green highlights, and the wine
opens cleanly with notes of toast and honey that anticipate
a well-structured whole. The domaine's Rosé 2002 Cuvée
Bérenger was also thought to be most accomplished.

**SCEA Preignes le Vieux, 34450 Vias,
tel. 04.67.21.67.82, fax 04.67.21.76.46,
e-mail preigneslevieux@aol.com
Tasting: ev. day except Sun. 8am–12 noon 1pm–6pm**

 € 3-5

DOMAINE DE SAINT-LOUIS 2001 ☆☆

14 hectares   30,000 bottles

The Domaine de Saint-Louis has its place in history by virtue of a dispute between Louis Pasteur, who visited in 1863, and the Privat family, who had recently developed a process to preserve wine by heating it. Pasteur went on to develop his "pasteurization" technique a year later. This lively 2001, with its wild fruit aromas and sustained bouquet, is a blend of Cabernet and Merlot, with an added touch of Syrah.

**Philippe Captier, Dom. de Saint-Louis, 34140 Loupian,
tel. 04.67.43.92.62, fax 04.67.43.70.80
Tasting: by appt.**

 € 5-8

LA SAUVAGEONNE 2001 ☆

3.6 hectares   12,000 bottles

This thiry-one-hectare domaine, acquired by new owners in 2001, is given over to Merlot and the two Cabernet grape varieties, all three of which are present in this 2001, with the lion's share going to Merlot. The red body and aromas of preserved fig, spices, and liquorice anticipate flavours that are full and generous, with tannins clearly present but kept firmly in their place, and never allowed to dominate.

**Dom. de La Sauvageonne, rte de Saint-Privat,
34700 Saint-Jean-de-la-Blaquière,
tel. 04.67.44.71.74, fax 04.67.44.71.02,
e-mail la-sauvageonne@wanadoo.fr
Tasting: by appt.**

 € 11-15

ROBERT SKALLI
Merlot 2001☆
17 hectares   120,000 bottles

Robert Skalli is recognized as having played a crucial role in developing the wines of southern France and his output always merits attention. This Merlot 2001 boasts a sustained garnet colour with amber highlights and a pungent nose redolent of spices and ripe fruit. The wine has softened somewhat, but not so as to weaken its intrinsically solid structure.

Les Vins Skalli, 278, av. du Mai.-Juin, BP 376, 34204 Sète Cedex, tel. 04.67.46.70.00, fax 04.67.46.71.99, e-mail info@vinskalli.com

 € 5-8

SOLSTICE
Merlot Réserve Barrique 2001☆☆
2 hectares   13,000 bottles

The Réserve Barrique 2001 is a youthful and sprightly garnet-coloured Merlot matured for ten months in both cask and vat. Its aromas suggest mild spices and mint, and its flavours on the palate are elegant and graceful, underpinned by unctuous tannins and sustained aromas.

Doms. du Soleil, Ch. Canet, 11800 Rustiques, tel. 04.90.12.30.22, fax 04.90.12.30.29

 € 5-8

CELLIER DU TERRAL
Cabernet Sauvignon 2001 ☆

5 hectares   5,000 bottles

The Cellier du Terral is a cellar cooperative that accommodates grape yields from 600 hectares, five hectares of which are given over to this deep purple-to-mauve Cabernet Sauvignon 2001, whose spicy aromas arise from vat rather than in-cask maturation. Mature and elegant tannins complement a wine that opens very strongly and develops well on the palate. This 2001 could be allowed to age a little before being served as an accompaniment to red meat.

Cellier du Terral, 34660 Cournonterral
Tasting: ev. day except Sat. Sun. 9am–12 noon 1.30pm–5pm

    € 3-5

DOMAINE TERRE GEORGES
Merlot 2001 ☆

1.06 hectares   7,500 bottles

Roland Coustal opened for business three years ago, when he took charge of this family owned domaine whose grapes had previously been processed by a cellar cooperative. The "Georges" featuring on the label of this Merlot 2001 is in honour of his wife Anne-Marie's father. Genealogy apart, the wine is good, very good. Although rather dark in colour (it is, when all is said and done, a Merlot), the wine is full of blackcurrant aromas. It opens forcefully, with pronounced and well-defined flavours and finishes on a positive note of cherry.

Anne-Marie et Roland Coustal, 2, rue de la Pinède,
11700 Castelnau-d'Aude,
tel. 06.30.49.97.73, fax 04.68.43.79.39
Tasting: by appt.

   € 5-8

DOMAINE DE TERRE MEGERE
Cabernet Sauvignon 2002☆☆

2 hectares   20,000 bottles

A deep purple Cabernet Sauvignon with violet highlights,
a pronounced nose and an opening that is full of character –
in short, a good wine in its category. This 2002 is vat-matured
and remarkably straightforward, with a flavourful fleshiness
that enhances the tasting pleasure. It remains to be said that
the *"mégère"* ("shrew") that features in the domaine name
has been well and truly tamed…

Michel Moreau, Dom. de Terre Mégère, Coeur de Village,
34660 Cournonsec,
tel. 04.67.85.42.85, fax 04.67.85.25.12,
e-mail terremegere@wanadoo.fr
Tasting: ev. day except Sun. 3pm–7pm; Sat. 9am–12.30pm

    €5-8

TERRES NOIRES
Sauvignon 2002☆

3 hectares   30,000 bottles

This Sauvignon 2002 boasts a clear, pale-straw colour and a
nose typical of the breed, together with aromatic properties
that are lively and sustained. The tasting jury also awarded
a star to the domaine's Colombard 2002 des Terres Noires.

Dominique Castillon, Dom. Les Terres Noires, 34450 Vias,
tel. 04.67.21.73.55, fax 04.67.21.68.38
Tasting: ev. day except Sat. Sun. 8am–12 noon 2pm–5pm

      €3-5

VERMEIL DU CRES
Muscat Sec 2002☆
4.68 hectares   26,000 bottles

A dry Muscat with a soft body and familiar fresh flavours on the palate. The same cooperative also produced a decidedly accomplished Vermeil du Crès Chardonnay 2002.

SCAV Vignerons de Sérignan, av. Roger-Audoux, 34410 Sérignan, tel. 04.67.32.24.82, fax 04.67.32.59.66
Tasting: ev. day except Sun. 9am–12 noon 3pm–6pm

DOMAINE DE LA VERNEDE
Merlot Les Artistes Création n° 2
Fût de Chêne 2001☆
5.18 hectares   2,400 bottles

The ecosystem of the Aude estuary plays host to a number of rare birds and this is surely one of them – a fiery purple Merlot 2001 that has been matured in oak casks for six months. Notes of leather and very ripe fruit – notably of unpicked cherries – stand out amid a host of flavours present in this well-structured, full, and balanced wine.

Jean-Marc Ribet, GAF de La Vernède, 34440 Nissan-lez-Ensérune, tel. 04.67.37.00.30, fax 04.67.37.60.11, e-mail chateaulavernede@infonie.fr
Tasting: ev. day 9am–1pm 3pm–7pm

DOMAINE VIGNE BLANCHE
Cabernet Sauvignon 2001☆☆

3 hectares   16,000 bottles

A highly coloured Cabernet Sauvignon 2001 from this
domaine on the limestone-flecked flanks of the irascible
Orbieu river, very close by the Abbaye de Fontfroide.
Pungent and complex aromas are the order of the day,
notably vanilla-flavoured spices and mature red fruit. Good
tannins contribute to an elegant and full-bodied structure. The
domaine's Domaine des Combes Rouge 2001 received one star.

**Vignerons de la Méditerranée, 12, rue du Rec-de-Veyret, ZI Plaisance,
BP 414, 11104 Narbonne Cedex,
tel. 04.68.42.75.00, fax 04.68.42.75.01,
e-mail rhirtz@listel.fr
Prop: E. Barsalou**

  € 5-8

WINTER HILL RESERVE
Chardonnay 2002☆

From the name on the label – Winter Hill Reserve – one
might almost be in Australia, and, as it happens, this cellar
adopts "Australian" methodology – harvesting the grapes at
night, rapid chilling, and so on. This very pale and very clear
Chardonnay 2002 represents good value. White flowers and
fresh fruit aromas dominate throughout. A light and delicate
wine that lives up to its provenance.

**UC Foncalieu, Dom. de Corneille, 11290 Arzens,
tel. 04.68.76.21.68, fax 04.68.76.32.01,
e-mail mkt@foncalieuvignobles.com
Prop: Cave des Coteaux de Saint-Cyr**

  € -3

DOMAINE LES YEUSES

Syrah Les Epices 2001 ☆

2.8 hectares   13,000 bottles

The domaine name "Yeuses" is somewhat deceptive, in that the word is commonly applied to a particular species of oak known variously as "holm" or "evergreen" (*Quercus ilex*), whereas the eighty-hectare property cultivated today by Jean-Paul and Michel Dardé is a tract of land lying between the foreshore and garrigue scrubland. This Syrah 2001 is distinguished by a purple-violet colour and by a relatively complex structure that is aromatic and sustained, hinting at flowers and leather. Overall, a pleasing combination.

Jean-Paul et Michel Dardé, Dom. Les Yeuses, rte de Marseillan, 34140 Mèze,
tel. 04.67.43.80.20, fax 04.67.43.59.32,
e-mail jp.darde@worldonline.fr
Tasting: ev. day except Sun. 9am–12 noon 3pm–7pm

 € 5-8

SABLES DU GOLFE DU LION

DOMAINE DE JARRAS
Gris de Gris 2002☆

40 hectares 400,000 bottles

Grenache, Carignan, and Cinsault grape varieties contribute in that order to this Gris de gris 2002, which confidently lives up to expectations. A pale body with copper highlights, and a nose and palate that are consistently fresh, aromatic, and sustained.

Domaines Listel, Ch. de Villeroy, BP 126, 34202 Sète Cedex, tel. 04.67.46.84.00, fax 04.67.46.84.55, e-mail jbonnardel@listel.fr
Tasting: ev. day 10am–5pm; cl. Sat. Sun. in winter

   € 3-5

DOMAINE DU PETIT CHAUMONT
Chardonnay 2002☆☆

8 hectares 10,000 bottles

Camargue bulls roam free about this domaine, where vines are dotted among the coastal sand dunes and a number of inland ponds – a clear illustration, perhaps, of the onerous circumstances under which this Chardonnay 2002 is produced. The vines appear to thrive under these conditions, however, yielding a wine that is refined and redolent of exotic fruits, with full and persistent flavours on the palate.

GAEC Bruel, Dom. du Petit Chaumont, 30220 Aigues-Mortes, tel. 04.66.53.60.63, fax 04.66.53.64.31, e-mail petitchaumont@netcourrier.com
Tasting: ev. day except Sun. 9am–12.30pm 3pm–7pm; groups by appt.

     € 5-8

Provence, the Lower Rhône Valley, and Corsica

The great majority of wines produced in the vast zone of Provence are reds, that amount to sixty per cent of the 900,000-hectolitre yield from the *départements* in the Provence-Alpes-Côte d'Azur (PACA) administrative region. Rosés (thirty per cent) are made mostly in Var, and whites come from Vaucluse and north of the Bouches-du-Rhône. A range of southern grapes is grown here, but they are rarely utilized on their own; depending on soil and climatic conditions, they are typically blended in varying proportions with grapes from other wine-growing regions, such as Chardonnay, Sauvignon, Cabernet or Merlot from Bordeaux, or Syrah from the Rhône Valley. Designations based on *départements* apply to Vaucluse, Bouches-du-Rhône, Var, Alpes-de-Haute-Provence, Alpes-Maritimes, and Hautes-Alpes; sub-regions include the Principality of Orange, Petite Crau (southeast of Avignon), Mont Caumes (west of Toulon), Argens (between Brignoles, and Draguignan in Var), Maures, Coteaux du Verdon (Var), the recently recognized Aigues (Vaucluse), and Corsica's Ile de Beauté. As of the 1999 harvest, wine denominated "Vin de Pays Portes de Méditerranée à Vocation Régionale" completes this category. Its area extends across the PACA region excluding Bouches-du-Rhône, Drôme, and Ardèche in the Rhône-Alpes.

LA MADELEINE
Cabernet Sauvignon 2002☆☆

8 hectares   15,000 bottles

A deep red nose and aromas of leather, dark berries and smokey notes characterize this Cabernet Sauvignon 2002. The finish reveals soft, well-rounded tannins complemented by a persistent flavour of red- and blackberries. This is an excellent wine to accompany a leg of lamb à la Provençale. The jury's attention was also drawn to a remarkable Marselan 2002 (a cross between Cabernet Sauvignon and Grenache Noir grapes), that, it was agreed, would be most appropriate with game.

**Pierre Bousquet, Cave la Madeleine, 04130 Volx,
tel. 04.92.72.13.91
Tasting: ev. day except Sun. 9am–12 noon 2pm–6.30pm**

    € 3-5

DOMAINE DE REGUSSE
Pinot Noir Elevé en Fût de Chêne 2001☆

A handsome Pinot Noir with an elegant vanilla nose and distinct wood notes that will attenuate over time, given the excellent overall balance and quality of this 2001. Raspberry aromas and subtle hints of vanilla add to the tasting pleasure. The jury also spoke well of the estate's oak cask matured Syrah 2002 Elevé en Fût de Chêne and its Muscat Moelleux 2002.

**Dieudonné, SARL Cave et Vignobles de Régusse,
rte de la Bastide-des-Jourdans, 04860 Pierrevert,
tel. 04.92.72.30.44, fax 04.92.72.69.08,
e-mail domaine-de-regusse@wanadoo.fr
Tasting: by appt.**

      € 5-8

DOMAINE DE ROUSSET
Viognier 2001☆

1 hectare   2,000 bottles

From Hubert and Roseline Emery comes this expressive
Viognier with flower (violet) notes and aromas of dried fruit
(apricot) that are clearly present on the palate. This appealing
wine is best allowed to breathe for a time before being served
either alone as an aperitif or with sweet and savoury dishes.

**Hubert et Roseline Emery, SCEV Ch. de Rousset, 04800 Gréoux-les-Bains,
tel. 04.92.72.62.49, fax 04.92.72.66.50
Tasting: by appt.**

    € 5-8

DOMAINE DE SAINT-JEAN 2002☆

10 hectares   5,000 bottles

The 2002 is a blend of Merlot and Cabernet Sauvignon
grapes. It gives off intense aromas of stewed fruit and is
silky on the palate, with flavours of red and dark fruit
(blackberries). The sound overall structure is an indication
that the grapes were harvested at optimal maturity.
Recommended as a wine to be served with a rack of lamb
with Provençal herbs and spices.

**Dom. de Saint-Jean, Chem. des Vannades, 04100 Manosque,
tel. 04.92.72.50.20, fax 04.92.87.84.01
Prop: d'Herbès**

 € 3-5

ALPES-MARITIMES

LOU VIN D'AQUI 2002 ☆☆ 🏆

0.4 hectares   3,900 bottles

The tasting panel was impressed with this white, made from the Provençal Rolle (or Vermentino) grape variety. The colour is clear and pale with green highlights and the wine opens with extremely delicate aromas of mild spices, fennel, and passion-fruit. The wine is ample on the palate and sustains spice and fruit notes through to an elegant finish. A wine that will hold its own with veal.

Nicolette de Toasc, 213, chem. de Crémat, 06200 Nice, tel. 04.92.15.14.14, fax 04.92.15.14.00
Tasting: by appt.

    € 5-8

ARGENS

TERROIR DU VAR

Gris ☆

87.5 hectares   700,000 bottles

A well-made and moderately priced light rosé that typically finds its way to supermarket shelves. This *vin gris* has an attractive colour and a nose that gives off notes of citrus fruits, notably grapefruit, that are sustained on the fresh and clean palate. A wine to be served with a cold buffet.

Les Celliers de Saint-Louis, Les Consacs, 83170 Brignoles, tel. 04.94.37.21.00, fax 04.94.59.14.84,
e-mail cellier-saintlouis@wanadoo.fr
Tasting: by appt.

      € -3

BOUCHES-DU-RHONE

DOMAINE DE L'ATTILON 2002☆

10 hectares   12,000 bottles

This 2001 is a pleasantly clear and luminous rosé with intense aromas of pulped wild strawberry and hints of boiled sweets. In short, a straightforward and refreshing wine that can be drunk either alone as an aperitif or as an accompaniment to a fish terrine or Provençal-style starter.

Comte de Roux, Dom. de L'Attilon, 13200 Arles,
tel. 04.90.98.70.04, fax 04.90.98.72.30,
e-mail de.roux.renaud@wanadoo.fr
Tasting: by appt.

    € 3-5

VIOGNIER DE LA GALINIERE

Viognier 2001☆☆ ♥

3.3 hectares   1,500 bottles

The finesse, power, and excellent balance of this Viognier 2001 found immediate favour with the tasting panel, not least because the apricot and toasted flavours imparted by the Viognier grape came through very strongly. A delightful prospect when served with duck foie gras.

Amédée-Laurent Musso, Ch. de la Galinière,
13790 Châteauneuf-le-Rouge,
tel. 04.42.29.09.84, fax 04.42.29.09.82,
e-mail chateaudelagaliniere@wanadoo.fr
Tasting: ev. day 9am–7pm

   € 15-23

DOMAINE DE L'ILE SAINT-PIERRE
Chardonnay 2002☆
30 hectares   50,000 bottles

A most successful Chardonnay distinguished by a brilliant body with green highlights, aromatic intensity with some honey notes, and a perfect balance on the palate. The wine finishes long on floral (honeysuckle) notes and is a model of harmony. Best, perhaps, with fish in a white sauce.

Marie-Cécile et Patrick Henry, Dom. de Boisviel-Saint-Pierre, 13104 Mas-Thibert, tel. 04.90.98.70.30, fax 04.90.98.74.93 Tasting: by appt.

 € 3-5

DOMAINE LA MICHELLE 2002☆☆ ♛
2 hectares   12,000 bottles

This rosé from the Vignerons du Garlaban is remarkable for its finesse and balanced structure. The wine is aromatic to a fault, with notes of fruit, hawthorn and broom which extend to a silk-like palate. The Caladoc Rosé 2002 des Vignerons du Garlaban also impressed the jury. Both wines are suggested as an ideal accompaniment to roast rabbit.

Dom. La Michelle, 13390 Auriol, tel. 04.42.04.40.63, fax 04.42.04.40.63, e-mail domainelamichelle@club-internet.fr Tasting: ev. day except Sun. Mon. 9am–12 noon 2pm–6pm

 € 5-8

MINNA VINEYARD 2000☆☆

2 hectares   5,900 bottles

A mastery of the vinification process and subsequent in-cask maturation. Complexity, sophisticated, with notes of vanilla. A wine to be enjoyed as of early 2004 – a genuine delight.

Villa Minna Vineyard, Roque Pessade CD 17, 13760 Saint-Cannat, tel. 04.42.57.23.19, e-mail villa.minna@wanadoo.fr
Tasting: ev. day except Sun. 9am–6pm Sat. 9am–1pm; cl. Aug.

   € 11-15

DOMAINE SAINT-VINCENT
Merlot-Cabernet 2002☆

3 hectares   12,000 bottles

The wine is a deep colour, with explosive ripe fruit and blackcurrant aromas. Well-rounded on the palate this is a bottle destined to prove a delicious accompaniment to a starter of aubergine caviar or a *pissaladière*.

P. et J.-P. Michel, GAEC Mas de Valériole, 13200 Arles, tel. 04.90.97.00.38, fax 04.90.97.01.78, e-mail phmichel@wanadoo.fr
Tasting: by appt.

 € 3-5

DOMAINE DE VALDITION
Cuvée Ludovic Dacla 2001☆

1.1 hectares   3,276 bottles

Distinguished by maturation in new casks; the wine mature more quickly. Also mentioned Cuvée des Filles Blanc 2002.

Dom. de Valdition, rte d'EygaFrères, 13660 Orgon, tel. 04.90.73.08.12, fax 04.90.73.05.95
Tasting: ev. day 9am–7pm

     € 15-23

DOMAINE VIRANT
Chardonnay 2002☆☆

3 hectares   6,000 bottles

Powerful, with grapefruit and lychee. Agreeable balance of citrus flavours and good finish. *See also* Cabernet 2002.

Robert Cheylan, Ch. Virant, CD 10, 13680 Lançon-de-Provence, tel. 04.90.42.44.47, fax 04.90.42.54.81, e-mail rcheylan@aol.com Tasting: by appt.

  € 3-5

WINES SELECTED BUT NOT STARRED

DOM. DES MASQUES
Chardonnay Philippe Cézanne Elevé en Fût de Chêne 2000

5 hectares   5,000 bottles

Didier et Magali Garçon, Dom. des Masques, 13100 Saint-Antonin-sur-Bayon, tel. 04.42.12.38.50, fax 04.42.12.38.50 Tasting: by appt.

€ 11-15

DOM. DE SURIANE 2002
17.64 hecatres   600 bottles

Marie-Laure Merlin, SCEA Dom. de Suriane, CD 10, 13250 Saint-Chamas, tel. 04.90.50.91.19, fax 04.90.50.92.80, e-mail mlmerlin@hotmail.com Tasting: ev. day except Sun. 9.30am–12.30pm 2pm–7.30pm

    € 3-5

COTEAUX DU VERDON

LA COLLINE DE VIGNELAURE
Merlot-Cabernet Sauvignon 1999☆☆

2 hectares   4,000 bottles

The jury responded with enthusiasm to this vintage, noting that in-cask maturation has not detracted from the wine's overall amplitude and roundness. Notes of vanilla and dark fruits are still distinctly present and seem likely to intensify and become more complex with time. Excellent with a fillet of beef en croûte. A cask-matured l'Esprit de Vignelaure Elevé en Fût Cabernet Sauvignon 2000 was also commended, on account of its classic structure and spicy aromas.

David O'Brien, Dom. Vignelaure, rte de Jouques, 83560 Rians,
tel. 04.94.37.21.10, fax 04.94.80.53.39,
e-mail vignelaure@wanadoo.fr
Tasting: ev. day 9.30am–1pm 2pm–6pm

   € 15-23

HAUTES-ALPES

DOMAINE ALLEMAND 2002☆
2 hectares   9,000 bottles

This clear, pale white from the Allemand estate met with approval on account of its aromatic intensity (citrus fruits, notably grapefruit) and its fresh and lively lemon notes on the palate. A most agreeable wine to accompany grilled fish. The tasting panel also singled out a rosé 2002 and a cask-matured Cuvée Vieilles Vignes Rouge 2001 made from the local Mollard grape.

EARL L. Allemand et Fils, La Plaine de Théus, 05190 Théus,
tel. 04.92.54.40.20, fax 04.92.54.41.50
Tasting: ev. day except Sun. 9am–12 noon 2pm–6pm

     € 3-5

DOMAINE DE TRESBAUDON 2001 ☆

2.3 hectares   10,000 bottles

This 2001 is made exclusively from Merlot, although the label does not specify the particular grape variety in question, merely identifying the wine by its estate name only. The wine has a relatively intense nose, with notes of liquorice, mint, and vanilla, and a fullness on the palate attributable to flavours of preserved fruit, pepper, and spices, that combine most agreeably.

Olivier Ricard, Les Lauzes, 05130 Tallard,
tel. 04.92.54.19.28, fax 04.92.54.17.67,
e-mail tresbaudon@wanadoo.fr
Tasting: by appt.

   € 5-8

ILE DE BEAUTE

DOMAINE AGHJE VECCHIE
Vecchio Pinot Noir 2001 ☆

1 hectare   4,000 bottles

In 2000, Florence Giudicelli started to work alongside her father at this estate, which was established in 1962 and now runs to close on eight hectares. The 2001 Pinot Noir deserves a mention, if for no other reason than its lustrous and clear ruby-red robe. That said, it has the added merits of powerful aromas typical of this grape variety and a balance and roundness accompanied by rich tannins. Suggestion: open one bottle now and save the others for later.

Jacques Giudicelli, Dom. Aghje Vecchie, 20230 Canale-di-Verde,
tel. 06.03.78.09.96, fax 04.95.38.03.37,
e-mail jerome.girard@attglobal.net
Tasting: by appt.

     € 5-8

CORSAIRE BLANC
Chardonnay 2002☆
80 hectares   500,000 bottles

An elegant freebooter of a wine with a yellow tone and green highlights, this 2002 exudes sustained aromas typical of the Chardonnay grape and achieves a balanced overall structure. A wine that can be enjoyed as of now. The Marestagno Rosé 2002, a blend of Grenache and Niellucciu varieties, was also awarded one star in recognition of its freshness and subtle aromas. A Les Polyphonies de Cépages Cabernet Sauvignon 2002 was also selected.

Union des Vignerons de l'Ile de Beauté,
Cave Coop. d'Aléria, 20270 Aléria,
tel. 04.95.57.02.48, fax 04.95.57.09.59,
e-mail barianichaba@aol.com
Tasting: by appt.

     €·3

DOMAINE DON PAOLU 2002☆
3.5 hectares   32,400 bottles

This 2002 is a yellow Vermentino with hints of green. It evokes flowers and a hint of aniseed, which are pronounced on the palate but quickly fade. A wine ready to drink now.

Cave Coop. d'Aghione, Samuletto, 20270 Aghione,
tel. 04.95.56.60.20, fax 04.95.56.61.27,
e-mail coop.aghionesamuletto@wanadoo.fr
Tasting: ev. day except Sat. Sun. 8.30am–12 noon 1.30pm–5.30pm

      € 3-5

MODERATO
Nectar d'Automne 2002☆☆
16.5 hectares   20,000 bottles

The 310 hectares of the Casabianca estate constitute the largest family owned domaine on the island. The estate's sweet Moderato, a *moelleux* made from Muscat à Petits Grains, found favour with the jury by virtue of its crystalline colour and gold highlights. Intense citrus and preserved fruit aromas sustain on the palate and an almost imperceptible sparkle "lifts" the wine and gives it remarkable balance. A wine to be enjoyed now or in a year's time. Another sweet Muscat from this estate, a Cantabilé Nectar d'automne 2002, was awarded one star.

**SCEA du Dom. Casabianca, 20230 Bravone,
tel. 04.95.38.96.08, fax 04.95.38.81.91,
e-mail domainecasabianca@wanadoo.fr**

   €8-11

MONTE E MARE 2002☆
25 hectares   200,000 bottles

The cooperative cellars of Saint-Antoine date from the mid-1970s. The jury awarded a star to a supple Gaspa Mora rouge 2002 with aromas of liquorice, as well as to this unctuous and fruity Monte e Mare, which should go well with meats with gravy.

**Cave de Saint-Antoine, Saint-Antoine, 20240 Ghisonaccia,
tel. 04.95.56.61.00, fax 04.95.56.61.60
Tasting: by appt.**

    €-3

DOMAINE DU MONT SAINT-JEAN
Pinot Noir 2002☆☆ 🏆

4.5 hectares   10,000 bottles

Set up in 1961 this domaine extends over ninty-five hectares
and is situated close to the beautiful village of Antisanti. It offers
an already most agreeable Pinot Noir, that will, beyond doubt,
improve over time: a dark-red colour, with generous and
predominantly floral aromas, shows spicy red fruit (cherries) on
the palate. Soft tannins contribute to a subtle overall balance. The
Aleatico 2002 selected boasts a deep-red hue and aromas typical
of the Muscat grape variety; it is a wine that deserves to be better
known. The tannic and persistent Merlot 2002 was also selected.

**Roger Pouyau, Dom. du Mont Saint-Jean, Campo Quercio,
BP 19 Antisanti, 20270 Aléria,
tel. 06.81.05.45.08, fax 04.95.38.50.29,
e-mail roger-pouyau@wanadoo.fr**
Tasting: by appt.

DOMAINE DE PETRAPIANA
Nielluciu 2002☆☆☆ 🏆

5 hectares   15,000 bottles

Ten out of ten for this superb deep-red Niellucciu, with its
complex aromas of lightly spiced red fruit, that tantalize the
nose and delight the palate. This subtle and impeccably structured
wine can be enjoyed now or laid down with confidence. Also
worth noting is the estate's vat-matured Merlot 2002, which is
awarded one star. A typical example of this grape variety, it will
benefit from ageing for one to three years.

**Eric Poli, Linguizzetta, 20230 San-Nicolao,
tel. 04.95.38.86.38, fax 04.95.38.94.71**
Tasting: by appt.

DOMAINE DE SALINE
Pinot Noir 2001☆☆

A continual winner. Dark-garnet-red colour; intense aromas; and good tannic structure, with length and balance for ageing. Perfect with game and red meat. Domaine de Terrazza Merlot 2002 received one star for its violet aromas and suppleness. Fleshy Domaine de Lischetto Chardonnay 2002, with a plethora of fruit aromas and flavours, was also selected.

Cave Coop. de la Marana, Rasignani, 20290 Borgo,
tel. 04.95.58.44.00, fax 04.95.38.38.10,
e-mail uval.sica@corsicanwines.com
Tasting: by appt.

DOMAINE TERRA VECCHIA 2002☆☆

Last year the white *vin de pays* 2001 won. This yea it is the red 2002 from Merlot, Cabernet Sauvignon, and Grenache. A clear, ruby-red wine that exudes intense aromas of red fruit, with a hint of iodine. Evokes a splendid array of pungent, long flavours on the palate. Excellent balance and harmony, for cellaring.

Coteaux de Diana, Dom. Terra Vecchia, Aléria, 20270 Tallone,
tel. 04.95.57.20.30, fax 04.95.57.08.98
Tasting: ev. day except Sat. Sun. 9am–1pm 2pm–6pm

WINE SELECTED BUT NOT STARRED

TERRA MARIANA
Merlot 2002

50 hectares   3,000,000 bottles

Uval, Rasignani, 20290 Borgo, tel. 04.95.58.44.00, fax
04.95.38.38.10, e-mail uval.sica@wanadoo.fr

MAURES

DOMAINE DE L'ANGLADE
Merlot 2002☆

2 hectares   13,500 bottles

A well-balanced Merlot, appreciated as an archetypal example
of the genre. The nose is expressive, with attractive floral
notes, and the overall impression is of a rounded and supple
wine full of character. Would be excellent in the company of a
daube Provençale. The estate's rosé 2002, made from Grenache
and Cinsault, also found favour with the jury.

**Bernard Van Doren, Dom. de l'Anglade, av. Vincent-Auriol,
83980 Le Lavandou,
tel. 04.94.71.10.89, fax 04.94.15.15.88,
e-mail dom.langlade@wanadoo.fr
Tasting: by appt.**

 € 5-8

LE GRAND CROS
Chardonnay L'Esprit de Provence 2002☆

1 hectare

A delightful Chardonnay with a nose redolent of spices,
brioche, and white-flesh fruit; open and straightforward
on the palate, with a judicious balance of peach and citrus
fruit flavours. Although the finish is on the short side, this
is a wine to be enjoyed, for example, with white fish baked
in an almond and honey crust.

**Famille Faulkner, Dom. du Grand Cros, D 13, 83660 Carnoules,
tel. 04.98.01.80.08, fax 04.98.01.80.09, e-mail info@grandcros.fr
Tasting: ev. day 9am–12 noon 2pm–7pm**

 € 5-8

MAROUINE
Carignan Vieilles Vignes 2001☆☆

0.9 hectares   3,800 bottles

Distinct and already complex aromas of red fruit; round and supple on the palate. Remarkable. A very attractive wine that will possibly age well, assuming one has the patience to allow it to do so.

Marie-Odile Marty, Ch. Marouïne, 83390 Puget-Ville,
tel. 04.94.48.35.74, fax 04.94.48.37.61
Tasting: ev. day except Sun. 9am–7pm

PASTOURETTE
Cabernet Sauvignon 2002☆

0.2 hectares   1,300 bottles

For those fortunate enough to lay their hands on this cherry-red 2002 rosé – nose and palate reveal aromas and flavours of red fruits. Fresh, fully rounded, and balanced.

SCA Cellier Saint-Bernard, av. du Général-de-Gaulle,
83340 Flassans-sur-Issole,
tel. 04.94.69.71.01, fax 04.94.69.71.80
Tasting: by appt.

WINE SELECTED BUT NOT STARRED
LONGUE TUBI
Cabernet Sauvignon 2002

0.6 hectares   5,000 bottles

Buisine, Dom. de Longue Tubi, 25, bd du Mas, 83700 Saint-Raphaël,
tel. 04.94.82.37.09, fax 04.94.19.27.03, e-mail cfb.viti@wanadoo.fr

MONT-CAUME

DOMAINE DU PEY-NEUF 2002☆

2.5 hectares   20,000 bottles

The cask-matured Vin de Pays du Mont-Caume Rouge 2001 was also mentioned.It is an accomplished red with distinct garrigue overtones, the white is attractive with clear floral notes and an unctuous, moreish impact on the palate, coupled with good length.

Guy Arnaud, 367, rte de Sainte-Anne, 83740 La Cadière-d'Azur, tel. 04.94.90.14.55, fax 04.94.26.13.89, e-mail guyarnaudvigneron5@wanadoo.fr
Tasting: by appt.

     € 3-5

PETITE CRAU

CELLIER DE LAURE
Cabernet Cuvée Pétrarque et Laure 2002☆

5.89 hectares   12,296 bottles

An excellent rosé obtained from a blend of robust red grape varieties, where the overall structure does not prejudice appreciation of the notes of fruit and nuanced spices. To be drunk with grilled chicken or a plate of pasta garnished with basil. Equally excellent is the cellar's Cuvée Prestige Rouge 2001, which should appeal to lovers of cask-matured wines.

SCA Cellier de Laure, 1, av. Agricol-Viala, 13550 Noves, tel. 04.90.94.01.30, fax 04.90.92.94.85, e-mail cellierdelaure@free.fr
Tasting: ev. day except Sun. 8am–12 noon 2pm–6.30pm

    € 3-5

PORTES DE MEDITERRANEE

DOMAINE LA BLAQUE
Pinot Noir 2001☆☆

9 hectares   48,000 bottles

Clear, dark-red, with subtle wood aromas. Finesse and elegance.

Gilles Delsuc, Dom. Châteauneuf-La Blaque, 04860 Pierrevert, tel. 04.92.72.39.71, e-mail domaine.lablaque@wanadoo.fr
Tasting: by appt.

    € 5-8

WINE SELECTED BUT NOT STARRED

CHARDONNAY DU PESQUIE 2002

3.86 hectares   6,000 bottles

SCEA Ch. Pesquié, rte de Flassan, BP 6, 84570 Mormoiron, tel. 04.90.61.94.08, e-mail chateaupesquie@yahoo.fr
Tasting: ev. day 9am–12 noon 2pm–6pm; cl. Sat. Sun. Oct.–Easter

  € 5-8

PRINCIPAUTE D'ORANGE

DYONYSOS
Viognier 2002☆

2.8 hectares   3,000 bottles

Clean and brilliant colour. Pungent nose of floral (violet) notes and liquorice. Opens forcefully, with fruit that softens gently.

EARL Dionysos, Chez M. Farjon, chem. du Marquis, 84100 Orange, tel. 04.90.34.46.31
Tasting: by appt.

     € 5-8

FONT SIMIAN 2002 ☆

2 hectares   12,000 bottles

Lively yet restrained, with finesse and hints of lemon.
Generously floral. Also mentioned is Numéro 2 de Jean-Pierre
Serguier Version 2003 Vin de Pays du Vaucluse Rouge.

Jean-Pierre Serguier, Ch. Simian, 84420 Piolenc,
tel. 04.90.29.50.67, e-mail chateau.simian@wanadoo.fr
Tasting: ev. day 8.30am–12.30pm 1.30pm–7.30pm

    € 3-5

VAR

DOMAINE DE GARBELLE
Vermentino 2002 ☆☆

0.75 hectares   1,500 bottles

Pale, clear, and very brilliant in colour. Aromas of pineapple,
citrus skins, and a hint of iodine. A well-balanced wine that
persists. Strongly recommended with scallops or sea bass.

Mathieu Gambini, Dom. de Garbelle, 83136 Garéoult,
tel. 04.94.04.86.30, fax 04.94.04.86.30
Tasting: ev. day 8.30am–12 noon 2pm–6pm

     € 5-8

WINE SELECTED BUT NOT STARRED

TRIENNES
Saint-Auguste 1999

15 hectares   50,000 bottles

Dom. de Triennes, RN 560, 83860 Nans-les-Pins,
tel. 04.94.78.91.46, triennes@wanadoo.com
Tasting: ev. day except Sun. 9am–12pm 1pm–6pm; groups by appt.

 € 5-8

THUERRY
Les Templiers de Villecroze 2000☆
1 hectare   6,000 bottles

An attractive 2000 with a very deep red colour, inherited no
doubt from the principal grape variety (Cabernet Sauvignon).
The mature grapes that went into this vintage have imparted
a roundness that sustains through a long finish. The nose
is fully open to reveal a variety of fruits. Perhaps best with
a leg of Provence lamb.

Ch. Thuerry, 83690 Villecroze,
tel. 04.94.70.63.02, fax 04.94.70.67.03,
e-mail thuerry@aol.com
Tasting: ev. day 9am–6.30pm (7.30pm in summer);
cl. Sun. from Apr. to Sep.   Prop: Croquet

    € 5-8

VAUCLUSE

DOMAINE DES ANGES
Chardonnay 2001☆
2.8 hectares   6,600 bottles

This sustained yellow Chardonnay develops subtle floral
aromas (white blossom) and unusual hints of broom and
caramel cream. Wood flavours remain decidedly pronounced.
The jury also selected the estate's Cabernet Sauvignon, a wine
matured in the cask for eleven months and distinguished by
a complex nose and an ample, woody palate.

Dom. des Anges, 84570 Mormoiron,
tel. 04.90.61.88.78, fax 04.90.61.98.05,
e-mail ciaranr@club-internet.fr
Tasting: ev. day 9am–12pm 2pm–6pm; 1 Oct.–1 Apr. by appt.

    € 5-8

DOMAINE DE LA BASTIDONNE
Chardonnay 2002☆
1.17 hectares   2,000 bottles

This fresh and, for want of a better word, pleasant Chardonnay 2000 is consistently light on the nose and palate, yet develops aromas of acacia blossom. The attack opens straightforward and convincing and the wine finishes round and long. Excellent as a stand-alone apéritif, but also recommended with a grilled sole or sea bream.

Gérard Marreau, SCEA Dom. de La Bastidonne,
84220 Cabrières-d'Avignon,
tel. 04.90.76.70.00, fax 04.90.76.74.34
Tasting: ev. day except Sun. 9am–12 noon 2pm–6pm

    € 5-8

DOMAINE BOUCHE
Sauvignon 2002☆
0.65 hectares   2,666 bottles

This light-gold Sauvignon 2000 with delicate floral aromas (white blossom) won over the jury. The tasting panel unanimously awarded it one star on discovering its freshness, balance and roundness on the palate, and its extended finish of flowers and peach notes. A classically harmonious Sauvignon that will go well with all manner of fish and seafood.

Dominique Bouche, chem. d'Avignon, 84850 Camaret-sur-Aigues,
tel. 06.62.09.27.19, fax 04.90.37.74.17
Tasting: by appt.

     € 5-8

DOMAINE DE LA CITADELLE
Cabernet Sauvignon 2002☆☆

4 hectares   16,000 bottles

A dark, almost black colour with brilliant violet highlights and a complex mix of blackberry, liquorice, pepper, and spice aromas, that are beautifully sustained on the palate through to a rounded and well-structured finish. This 2002 is a credit to the winemaker and a rare delight to the wine-lover as an accompaniment to grilled sirloin – now or at any time up to 2005.

Rousset-Rouard, Dom. de la Citadelle, rte de Cavaillon, 84560 Ménerbes, tel. 04.90.72.41.58, fax 04.90.72.41.59, e-mail domainedelacitadelle@wanadoo.fr
Tasting: ev. day 10am–12 noon 2pm–6pm; cl. Sun. from Nov. to Mar.; groups by appt.

 € 3-5

DOMAINE FONDACCI
Chasan 2002☆☆🏆

2.5 hectares   10,000 bottles

It proved necessary to choose between two Chasan grape-based wines presented by Guy Fondacci. The oak-cask-matured 2001 Elevé en Fût de Chêne was adjudged remarkable, but the 2002 stole the show on the strength of the exceptional level of quality, expertise, and commitment demonstrated by a winemaker confronted by what tended to be a problematic vintage. The wine has splendid aromas of exotic fruits that persist through to a protracted finish. This wine is a delight, even more so when enjoyed as an accompaniment to sweet and savoury dishes.

Dom. Guy Fondacci, quartier La Sablière, 84580 Oppède, tel. 04.90.76.95.91, fax 04.90.71.40.38, e-mail guyfondacci@aol.com
Tasting: ev. day 10.30am–12 noon 2.30pm–18pm

 € 3-5

DOMAINE FONTAINE DU CLOS
Chardonnay 2002☆☆

4 hectares   5,000 bottles

Remarkable. Intense white-flesh fruit, structured roundness, with distinct flavours of peaches in syrup and a long finish.

**EARL Jean Barnier, Dom. Fontaine du Clos, 84260 Sarrians,
tel. 04.90.65.42.73, fax 04.90.65.30.69, e-mail cave@fontaineduclos.com
Tasting: ev. day except Sun. 9am–12 noon 3pm–7pm**

 € 3-5

DOMAINE GRAND CALLAMAND
Merlot 2000☆

1 hectare   6,000 bottles

Expressive; deep-red, almost black. Generous aromas of moccha, toast, and liquorice. Full and sustained (with pronounced wood).

**Dom. Grand Callamand, rte de la Loubière, 84120 Pertuis,
tel. 04.90.09.61.00, e-mail chateau-grandcallamand@wanadoo.fr
Tasting: by appt.**

 € 5-8

DOMAINE DE MAROTTE
Viognier 2002☆☆☆ ♆

2 hectares   4,000 bottles

Exceptional Viognier from a difficult year. Expressive wine. The nose offers apricot blossom and quince that carry through to the finish. Also mentioned is the Vin de Pays de Vaucluse Rosé 2002.

**Dom. de Marotte, petit chemin de Serres, 84200 Carpentras,
tel. 04.90.63.43.27, fax 04.90.67.15.28, e-mail marotte@wanadoo.fr
Tasting: ev. day except Mon. 8.30am–12 2.30pm–6.30pm; cl. Jan. and Feb.**

 € 5-8

DOMAINE MEILLAN-PAGES
Sauvignon 2002☆

1.57 hectares   6,000 bottles

Fruity and harmonious. Also mentioned is the Cabernet 2001.

**Dom. Meillan-Pagès, quartier La Garrigue, 84580 Oppède,
tel. 04.32.52.17.50, fax 04.90.76.94.78, e-mail meillan@terre-net.fr
Tasting: ev. day 10am–8pm**

WINES SELECTED BUT NOT STARRED

DOM. DU COULET ROUGE
Cabernet 2002

2 hectares   8,000 bottles

**Dom. du Coulet Rouge, Les Bâtiments Neufs, 84220 Roussillon,
tel. 04.90.05.61.40, fax 04.90.05.61.40
Tasting: ev. day 8am–12 noon 1.30pm–7pm**

LASKAR 2001

4 hectares   15,114 bottles

**SCA les Vins de Sylla, 178, quartier du Viaduc, BP 141, 84405 Apt Cedex,
tel. 04.90.74.05.39, fax 04.90.04.72.06**

DOM. DE LA VERRIERE VIOGNIER
Elevé en Fût de Chêne 2002

1.25 hectares   5,300 bottles

**Jacques Maubert, Dom. de La Verrière, 84220 Goult,
tel. 04.90.72.20.88, e-mail laverriere2@wanadoo.fr
Tasting: ev. day except Sun. 9am–12 noon 2pm–6pm**

The Alps and the Southeast

This region extends from Auvergne to the Alps and includes the eight *départements* of the Rhône-Alps and the Puy-de-Dôme. The terroir is exceptionally disparate, that results in a range of regional wines. Burgundy varieties (Pinot, Gamay, Chardonnay) grow side-by-side with southern varieties such as Grenache, Cinsault, and Clairette, and other regional varieties such as Syrah, Roussanne, and Marsanne in the Rhône Valley, together with Mondeuse, Jacquère or Chasselas in Savoie, and Etraire de la Dui and Verdesse from Val d'Isère). Bordeaux varieties also exist, notably Merlot, Cabernets, and Sauvignon. Production is on the increase and is approaching 400,000 hectolitres. Ardèche and Drôme produce the majority of the reds. The five departments are Ain, Ardèche, Drôme, Isère, and Puy-de-Dôme; eight regionss are Allobrogie (Savoie and Ain, 7,000 hectolitres – mostly white), Coteaux du Grésivaudan (central Isère, 1,500 hectolitres), Balmes Dauphinoises (Isère, 1,000 hectolitres), Urfé (Loire Valley: Forez to Roannais, 2,000 hectolitres), Collines Rhodaniennes (20,000 hectolitres, mostly red), Comté de Grignan (southwest of Drôme, 25,000 hectolitres, mostly red), Coteaux des Baronnies (southeast of Drôme, 25,000 hectolitres, only red), and Coteaux de l'Ardèche (300,000 hectolitres of red, white, and rosé). In addition come two regions: Vin de Pays des Comtés Rhodaniens (5,000 hectolitres) – that can perhaps also be produced in the eight Rhône-Alpes *départements* (Ain, Ardèche, Drôme, Isère, Loire, Rhône, Savoie, Haute-Savoie); and a Vin de Pays Portes de Méditerranée, that applies to Provence-Alpes-Côte d'Azur (PACA), Drôme, and Ardèche.

DOMAINE DEMEURE-PINET
Jacquère 2002☆☆ 🏆

3.5 hectares   30,000 bottles

This remarkable and beautifully pale-yellow Jacquère 2002
is a fine example from the Demeure-Pinet estate. The wine
exudes delicate and subtle aromas of white flowers, honey,
apricot, and lime. It is fresh, lively, and slightly sparkling
on the palate, with a broad palette of flavours ranging
from citrus fruits to newly mown grass. This is a highly
accomplished and true-to-type Jacquère that will do full
justice to freshwater fish. Also from this estate, the jury
selected a Chardonnay 2002, which proved to be a very
well-balanced and attractively rounded wine, one that holds
on the palate with flavours of ripe white fruit.

**Le Cellier de Joudin, Dom. Demeure-Pinet-Joudin,
73240 Saint-Genix-sur-Guiers,
tel. 04.76.31.61.74, fax 04.76.31.61.74
Tasting: ev. day except Sun. pm**

DOMAINE DE CHAMPAL
Viognier Arzelle 2002☆☆

3.7 hectares   8,000 bottles

This is the most promising of Viogniers, an Arzelle 2002 with a pale-white appearance and hints of silver. This harmonious wine gives off aromas of flowers and white fruit. It is still young, however, and will benefit from a year in the cellar before being enjoyed together with a spring salad.

Eric Rocher, Dom. de Champal, quartier Champal, 07370 Sarras, tel. 04.78.34.21.21, fax 04.78.34.30.60, e-mail vignobles-rocher@wanadoo.fr
Tasting: by appt.

   € 8-11

DOMAINE DU CHATEAU VIEUX 2001☆

0.09 hectares   900 bottles

This estate has been a standard-bearer of winemaking in the Drôme for no less than five generations. This 2001 from the cellars of the eighteenth century Domaine du Château Vieux comes in the guise of a most handsome Syrah matured in oak casks, a decidedly individualistic wine with a dark-red robe and a nose that exudes aromas of ripe fruit. On the palate, flavours of spice and hints of vanilla make their presence felt against a backdrop of fine, elegant, and softening tannins. A wine to be discovered with poultry – chicken in a vanilla sauce, perhaps?

Fabrice Rousset, Le Château Vieux, 26750 Triors, tel. 04.75.45.31.65, fax 04.75.71.45.35, e-mail domainechateauvieux@chez.com
Tasting: by appt.

   € 5-8

COLLINES RHODANIENNES

WINE SELECTED BUT NOT STARRED

CAVE DE TAIN L'HERMITAGE

Marsanne Nobles Rives 2002

105,000 bottles

Cave de Tain-l'Hermitage, 22, rte de Larnage, BP 3, 26601
Tain-l'Hermitage Cedex,
tel. 04.75.08.20.87, e-mail commercial.france@cave-tain-hermitage.co

    € 3-5

COMTE DE GRIGNAN

WINE SELECTED BUT NOT STARRED

CAVE DE LA VALDAINE

Cabernet Sauvignon 2002

36.3 hectares   6,600 bottles

SCA Cave de la Valdaine, av. Max-Dormoy, 26160 Saint-Gervais-sur-Roubion,
tel. 04.75.53.80.08, e-mail cave.valdaine@free.fr

    € -3

COTEAUX DE L'ARDECHE

CAVE COOPERATIVE D'ALBA

Pinot Noir Sélection 2001☆

2 hectares   10,000 bottles

Violet, kirsch, cherry, ginger-bread, and vanilla. Supple yet robust.

Cave Coop. d'Alba, La Planchette, 07400 Alba-la-Romaine,
tel. 04.75.52.40.23, fax 04.75.52.48.76, e-mail cave.alba@free.fr
Tasting: ev. day except Sun. 9am–12 noon 1.30pm–6pm; sum. 2pm–7pm

     € 5-8

LES VIGNERONS ARDECHOIS
Viognier Prestige 2001 ☆☆

Twenty-five cooperatives in the Ardèche region claim to have
met the challenge first – to put quality wines from the region
firmly on the map. This remarkable wine fully merits its
rating: pungent, balanced, and full of pedigree, it gives off
delightful aromas of peach and apricot and exhibits excellent
length and body on the palate. One star was awarded to the
Merlot Prestige 2001, harmonious, elegantly powerful, and
with an attractive nose of red fruit, floral, and balsamic notes.
One star was also awarded to the red Cuvée Prestige 1999.

Les Vignerons Ardéchois, quartier Chaussy, 07120 Ruoms,
tel. 04.75.39.98.00, fax 04.75.39.69.48,
e-mail uvica@uvica.fr
Tasting: by appt.

 € 3-5

DOMAINE DE BOURNET
Cuvée Chris 2000 ☆☆
6 hectares   12,000 bottles

A magnificent seventeenth century *mas* situated among the
gorges of the Ardèche lies at the hub of this family owned
domaine, that routinely turns out highly original wines full
of character. The Cuvée Chris 2000 is a blend of Cabernet and
Merlot matured in oak casks for twelve months, a seductive
wine with a deep-red colour, an expressive nose of spices and
mineral notes, and a perfect overall balance and power. This is
a wine that can be laid down almost indefinitely.

GAEC Dom. de Bournet, 07120 Grospierres,
tel. 04.75.39.68.20, fax 04.75.39.06.96,
e-mail domaine.debournet@advalvas.be
Tasting: ev. day 9am–12 noon 2pm–6pm

 € 8-11

GRAND ARDECHE
Chardonnay 2001☆☆
50 hectares 250,000 bottles

The celebrated Burgundy house of Louis Latour opted in 1979 for the Ardèche as an appropriate area in which to produce top-of-the-range Chardonnay *vins de pays*. The gamble has paid off, due in no small part to redoubtable Latour expertise and knowhow. This Chardonnay 2001 is a shining example: an inordinately rich wine matured for ten months in oak casks to yield a pungent yet elegant nose, with subtle notes of spice, vanilla, exotic fruits, and honey. A thoroughbred in every sense, powerful and fleshy, that should be cellared for at least two years before being enjoyed in conjunction with a fillet of turbot or grilled fowl.

Maison Louis Latour, La Téoule, 07400 Alba-la-Romaine, tel. 04.75.52.45.66, fax 04.75.52.87.99

   € 8-11

DOMAINE DES LOUANES
L'Encre de Sy 2002☆☆
1.23 hectares 800 bottles

This family owned estate in the commune of Balazuc is run on organic lines. The Encre de Sy 2002 is a Syrah that boasts a dark red, virtually black body with notes of violet and a nose bursting with aromas of ripe fruit. A powerful and well-balanced wine that promises to age well over the next one to three years, before being served with game dishes.

**Jérôme Poudevigne, Les Louanes, 07120 Balazuc, tel. 04.75.37.75.09, fax 04.75.37.75.09, e-mail claforet@netcourrier.com
Tasting: by appt.**

       € 5-8

MAS DE BAGNOLS
Chardonnay 2002☆
0.66 hectares   2,500 bottles

The nose is well-advanced, with mineral notes and fruit and spices. On the palate, its true aromatic complexity shows dried fruit and spice. Fresh and rounded wine for grilled fish.

Pierre Mollier, Mas de Bagnols, 07110 Vinezac,
tel. 04.75.36.83.10, fax 04.75.36.98.04
Tasting: ev. day except Sun. 8am–12 noon 2pm–6pm

   € 5-8

MAS D'INTRAS
Cabernet Sauvignon 2000☆☆♙
1.6 hectares   13,000 bottles

"Powerful", "robust", and "expressive", with concentrated aromas of spice and musk. Also selected was the estate's full and fleshy Syrah 2001, and Grenache-based *cuvée* Trace Nègre.

Denis et Emmanuel Robert, Mas d'Intras, 07400 Valvignères,
tel. 04.75.52.75.36, fax 04.75.52.51.62, e-mail contact@masdintras.fr
Tasting: ev. day 9.30am–12 noon 1.30pm–6.30pm;
Sun. 1.30pm–6.30pm only

 € 5-8

WINES SELECTED BUT NOT STARRED
CAVE COOPERATIVE DE MONTFLEURY
Syrah 2002
30 hectares   58,000 bottles

Cave Coop. de Montfleury, quartier Gare, 07170 Villeneuve-de-Berg,
tel. 04.75.94.82.76, fax 04.75.94.89.45
Tasting: by appt.

   €-3

CAVE COOPERATIVE DE VALVIGNERES
Viognier 2002

50 hectares   10,000 bottles

**Cave Coop. de Valvignères, quartier Auvergne, 07400 Valvignères,
tel. 04.75.52.60.60,e-mail cave.valvigneres@free.fr**

    €-3

COTEAUX DES BARONNIES

DOMAINE DU RIEU FRAIS
Cabernet Sauvignon Cuvée Alexandre 2000☆☆

3 hectares   19,000 bottles

Dark-red with hints of blue, the nose is discreet and complex,
with peppers and spices. Elegant soft tannins that mingle with
spice and ripe fruit flavours. Balanced and elegant.

**Jean-Yves Liotaud, quartier du Rieux-Frais, 26110 Sainte-Jalle,
tel. 04.75.27.31.54, e-mail jean-yves.liotaud@wanadoo.fr
Tasting: ev. day 9am–12 noon 2pm–6pm; cl. Sun. Nov.–Feb.**

    € 5-8

DOMAINE LA ROSIERE
Merlot 2001☆☆🏆

5 hectares   20,000 bottles

Excellent pedigree and structure, together with its concentrated
aromas, ranging from blueberries to blackcurrants by way of
mineral notes and spices. Round and fleshy, with flavours of black
fruit and musk. Balanced and exceptionally harmonious.

**EARL Serge Liotaud et Fils, Dom. La Rosière, 26110 Sainte-Jalle,
tel. 04.75.27.30.36, e-mail vliotaud@yahoo.fr
Tasting: ev. day 9am–7pm**

     € 3-5

DOMAINE DE ROUSTILLAN
Cuvée Fruitée 2001☆

15 hectares

The Domaine de Roustillan boasts twenty-five years'
experience of organic cultivation. This deep garnet-red 2001,
made from a blend of Grenache, Merlot, Gamay, and Syrah
grapes, is aromatically complex, mixing red fruits with traces
of vanilla. The wine opens on a note of fresh fruit. Balanced
and robust, it is perhaps best suited to being drunk as a
partner to game dishes.

**Frédéric Alaïmo, Dom. de Roustillan, 26170 La Penne-sur-Ouréze,
tel. 04.75.28.09.58, fax 04.75.28.12.49,
e-mail domaine.de.roustillan@wanadoo.fr
Tasting: ev. day 10am–2pm 3pm–7pm; Sun. 3pm–7pm only**

  € 3-5

DROME

DOMAINE LE PLAN 2001☆
1.77 hectares   16,000

Dirk Vermeersch works out of an eighteenth century
Provençal *mas* to produce this intense 2001 red, with its
pronounced aromas of ripe-red fruit and spices. The wine
emerges balanced and rounded on the palate, with flavours
of stewed red fruit against a background of softened tannins.
A wine to be reserved for grilled meat dishes.

**Dom. Le Plan-Vermeersch, Le Plan, 26790 Tulette,
tel. 04.75.98.36.84,
e-mail dva@domaine-leplan.com
Tasting: ev. day 10am–12 noon 3pm–6pm; cl. 11 Nov.–31 Mar.**

   € 5-8

The Northeast

The modest remnants of vines decimated by phylloxera in the ninteenth century are to be found in this area of France. These are vines that had their hour of glory – or glory reflected, as it happens, from their prestigious neighbours in Burgundy and in Champagne. Grape varieties from those two regions are still cultivated here, together with vines originating in Alsace and the Jura. For the most part, these are vinified singly and, as a result, generally reflect the individual character of their provenance: Auxerrois, Chardonnay, Pinot Noir, Gamay or Pinot Gris.

Vins de pays from Franche-Comté, Meuse, Saône-et-Loire, Haute-Marne or Yonne are all, virtually without exception, light, fresh, and aromatic. Although yields are increasing, notably in respect of white wine varieties, total annual production still stands at around a mere 9,000 hectolitres, of which whites represent 5,000 hectolitres and reds 3,000 hectolitres.

COTEAUX DE L'AUXOIS

VIGNOBLE DE FLAVIGNY
Chardonnay Fût de Chêne 2001☆☆ 🏆

2.5 hectares 5,000 bottles

It is only ten years since the first "new" stocks were planted here in this fifteen-hectare vineyard at Flavigny in the Côte d'Or. What better way to celebrate this renaissance, then, than with this Chardonnay 2001, an unctuous buttered toast of a wine which opens fresh and subsequently releases flavours of honey and almonds? Also recommended is an Auxerrois 2002 with attractive notes of quince and a rounded body.

Ida Nel, SCEA Vignoble de Flavigny, Dom. du Pont Laizan, 21150 Flavigny-sur-Ozerain, tel. 03.80.96.25.63, fax 03.80.96.25.63, e-mail vignoble-de-flavigny@wanadoo.fr
Tasting: by appt.

    € 5-8

VILLAINES-LES-PREVOTES-VISERNY
Cuvée Tradition 2002☆

Intrepid pioneering winemakers settled here between Semur and Montbard in the Côte d'Or and planted speculative vines that are now starting to yield good results, as this yellow-bodied and modestly aromatic blend of Chardonnay (60%), Pinot Gris (25%), and Auxerrois (15%) demonstrates. Hints of fruit emerge on the palate as the different grape varieties gradually release their respective flavours. A full and well-structured wine.

SA des Coteaux de Villaines-les-Prévôtes-Viserny, 21500 Villaines-les-Prévôtes, tel. 03.80.96.71.95, fax 03.80.96.71.95, e-mail vins.villainesviserny@wanadoo.fr
Tasting: by appt.

    € 3-5

COTEAUX DE COIFFY

LES COTEAUX DE COIFFY
Auxerrois 2002☆

4 hectares   15,000 bottles

These vines grow in Haute-Marne, not far from the thermal
baths of Bourbonne-les-Bains. After half a century of enforced
hibernation, this fifteen-hectare vineyard has re-emerged and
is gradually starting to make its mark. The golden yellow
Auxerrois 2002 appeals to the eye, nose and palate. Fruit aromas
predominate, together with a hint of mint, and sustain on the
palate in a wine that opens lively and rounds out well. The
vineyard's Pinot Gris 2002 was also selected on the strength
of its ripe fruit flavours.

**Renaut-Camus, SCEA les Coteaux de Coiffy, 52400 Coiffy-le-Haut,
tel. 03.25.84.80.12, fax 03.25.90.18.84,
e-mail renautlaurent@aol.com
Tasting: ev. day 2.30pm–6pm**

FRANCHE-COMTE

VIGNOBLE GUILLAUME
Chardonnay Collection Réservée 2001☆☆🏆

1 hectare   5,000 bottles

Back in the Middle Ages, this vineyard in the Haute-Saône
belonged to the archbishops of Besançon. The Guillaume
family – in the wine business "only" since the eighteenth
century – now cultivates this thirty-three-hectare property
and also grows vinestocks for export to the four corners of the
world. The jury enjoyed a cask-matured Pinot Noir Collection
Réservée and felt it worthy of a star, but waxed eloquent over
this Chardonnay 2001, with its brilliantly clear and consistent

colour and bouquet of honey and brioche. Wood flavours are still present after time spent in the cask, but toasted notes assert themselves on the palate and a hint of sparkle lifts this mature, well-rounded, and concentrated vintage.

Vignoble Guillaume, rte de Gy, 70700 Charcenne, tel. 03.84.32.80.55, fax 03.84.32.84.06, e-mail vignoble.guillaume@wanadoo.fr Tasting: by appt.

  € 15-23

PASCAL HENRIOT
Auxerrois Coteaux de Champlitte 2001☆
1.5 hectares 3,300 bottles

Champlitte in the Haute-Saône near the Côte d'Or is a monument to rural tradition, exemplified by its attractive museum of country life and, not least, by the vines that were replanted here thirty years ago by Pascal Henriot, a wine-grower who works organically under the watchful eye of Ecocert. Pascal is to be congratulated on this excellent light gold Auxerrois 2001, with an expressive nose of ripe fruit and subtle suggestions of honey. In short, an attractively textured wine with pronounced aromatic qualities.

Pascal Henriot, 5, rue des Capucins, 70600 Champlitte, tel. 03.84.67.68.85, e-mail pascal.henriot2@wanadoo.fr Tasting: by appt.

 € 3-5

LE MUID MONTSAUGEONNAIS
Pinot Noir Elevé en Fût de Chêne 2001 ☆☆☆ 🏆

1.9 hectares   14,200 bottles

Situated near the Côte d'Or. In 1988, Vaux and Montsaugeon pooled resources to restore this vineyard. Twelve hectares yield excellent results, in particular this marvellous Pinot Noir 2001. Garnet-red, with a complex, refined nose of griotte cherries and bilberries, it is full, concentrated, and pungent; irreproachably solid, with fine tannins. Vat-matured Pinot Noir 2002 Elevé en Cuvée boasts a robustness that augurs well.

Le Muid Montsaugeonnais, 23, av. de Bourgogne, 52190 Vaux-sous-Aubigny, tel. 03.25.90.04.65, fax 03.25.90.04.65, e-mail muidmontsaugeonnais@wanadoo.fr
Tasting: by appt.

 € 5-8

MEUSE

L'AUMONIERE
Vin Gris 2002 ☆

4,600 bottles

Auxerrois, Chardonnay, and Pinot Noir make up this wine from a 5.6-hectare property near Lake Madine. Light, salmon-pink in colour; it is aromatic and flavourful, soft and fruity with a long finish. The vineyard itself was established as recently as 1984; on the strength of this 2002, however, it is already making its mark.

L'Aumonière, Viéville-sous-les-Côtes, 55210 Vigneulles-les-Hattonchâtel, tel. 03.29.89.31.64, fax 03.29.90.00.92

 € .3

DOMAINE DE COUSTILLE
Gris 2002☆☆
1 hectare   5,200 bottles

Dark pink; admirably round from colour to finish. Agreeable wine – well-structured, fruity and persistent on the palate.

N. Philippe, SCEA de Coustille, 23, Grand-Rue, 55300 Buxerulles, tel. 03.29.89.33.81, e-mail n.philippe@domaine-de-coustille.com Tasting: by appt.

LAURENT DEGENEVE
Auxerrois 2002☆☆ ♈
0.5 hectares   3,800 bottles

Two wines were selected – salmon-pink Gris 2002 with good aromas and structure, and this "custom-built", pale-yellow white wine. Richly aromatic and exotic on the palate. Flavours of grapefruit and lime last through to a long, balanced finish.

Laurent Degenève, 7, rue des Lavoirs, 55210 Creuë, tel. 03.29.89.30.67, e-mail laurent.degeneve@wanadoo.fr Tasting: by appt.

DOMAINE DE LA GOULOTTE
Gris 2002☆
1 hectare   7,000 bottles

Red-fruit aromas reflect the Gamay (80%) and Auxerrois. Lively with a most creditable finish.

EARL Dom. de la Goulotte, 6, rue de l'Eglise, 55210 Saint-Maurice, tel. 03.29.89.38.31, fax 03.29.90.01.80 Tasting: by appt.

DOMAINE DE MUZY
Pinot Noir 2001☆
2 hectares   8,000 bottles

A rich, ruby-red Pinot with a peppery nose and pleasing wood notes. An ample, fleshy wine with soft tannins.

Véronique et Jean-Marc Liénard, Dom. de Muzy, 3, rue de Muzy, 55160 Combres-sous-les-Côtes,
tel. 03.29.87.37.81, e-mail muzylienard@wanadoo.fr
Tasting: by appt.

    € 3-5

SAINTE-MARIE-LA-BLANCHE

WINE SELECTED BUT NOT STARRED
BLANCHE
Chardonnay 2001
2.5 hectares   26,000 bottles

Les Caves des Hautes-Côtes, rte de Pommard, 21200 Beaune,
tel. 03.80.25.01.00, e-mail vinchc@wanadoo.fr
Tasting: by appt.

   € 3-5

YONNE

WINE SELECTED BUT NOT STARRED
DOM. LA FONTAINE AUX MUSES
Pinot Noir 2002
0.5 hectares   3,000 bottles

Vincent Pointeau-Langevin, La Fontaine aux Muses, 89116 La Celle-Saint-Cyr, tel. 03.86.73.40.22, e-mail fontaineauxmuses@aol.com

   € 5-8

INDEX

Acacias, Dom. les 47
Acacias, Dom. les 47
Adea Consules 13
Agenais 31–2
Aghje Vecchie, Dom. 111
Aigues Belles, Dom. d' 76
Alba, Cave Coopérative d' 129
Allemand, Dom. 110
Allobrogie 127
Alpes-de-Haute-Provence 103–4
Alpes-Maritimes 105
Alpes et Pays Rhodaniens 126–34
Anges, Dom. des 121
Anglade, Dom. de l' 116
Aquitaine and Charentes 30–42
Ardailloux, Dom. des 53
Ardèche 128
Argens 105
Arjolle, Dom. de l' 68
Attilon, Dom. de l' 106
Aude 55
Augeron, Dom. d' 42
Aumônière, L' 139

Bagnols, Mas de 132
Bastidonne, Dom. de la 122
Baubiac, Dom. de 76
Baume, Dom. de la 77
Baux, Mas 58
Beausejour Judell, Dom. de 77
Beauvignac, Hugues de 67
Bénovie 56
Bergerie d'Amilhac, Dom. de la 78
Blanche 141
Blaque, Dom. la 119
Bordes, Dom. de 31
Bosc, Le 78
Bouche, Dom. 122

Bouches-du-Rhône 106–9
Boudau, Dom. 65
Bouis, Dom. le 79
Bournet, Dom. de 130
Bouscas, Dom. le 47
Bouysse, Dom. de la 55
Brard Blanchard 33
Bruneau, Dom. 33

Calvet de Calvet 79
Camas 80
Camentron, Dom. de 42
Camp-Galhan, Dom. 80
Campet, Dom. de 32
Caprice de Colombelle 47
Cassagnoles, Dom. des 48
Cassan 56–7
Catalan 58
Cathare 59
Causses de Nizas 59
Caux 59
Cazeaux, Dom. de 31
Cévennes 60
Chai du Rouissoir 34
Chambert, Dom. de 81
Champal, Dom. de 128
Charentais 33–8
Charmettes, Dom. les 81
Château d'Eau, Dom. du 82
Château Vieux, Dom. du 128
Chauvillière, Dom. de la 34
Cher 12
Chevrières, Dom. des 14
Ciffre, Dom. de 63
Cigalus 82
Citadelle, Dom. de la 123
Clapière, Dom. de la 83
Coche, Dom. de la 14
Collier de la Toison d'or 50
Colline de Vignelaure, La 110

Collines de la Moure 60
Collines Rhodaniennes 129
Colombette, Dom. de la 62
Comte de Grignan 129
Comte de Laudonnière 14
Comté Tolosan 44–5
Condamine Bertrand 84
Cormerais, Dom. Bruno 15
Corrèze 45
Corsaire Blanc 112
Corsica 102
Coteaux de l'Ardèche 129–33
Coteaux de l'Auxois 136
Coteaux des Baronnies 133–4
Coteaux de Chalosse 40
Coteaux Charitois 12
Coteaux de Coiffy, Les 137
Coteaux des Fenouillèdes 61
Coteaux du Libron 62
Coteaux du Mezinais 53
Coteaux de Murviel 63
Coteaux et Terrasses de Montauban 46
Coteaux du Verdon 110
Côtes Catalanes 64–5
Côtes du Condomois 46
Côtes de Gascogne 47–51
Côtes de Pérignan 66
Côtes du Tarn 51–2
Côtes de Thau 67
Côtes de Thongue 68–70
Couchetière, Dom. de la 15
Coujan, Dom. de 63
Coulet Rouge, Dom. de 125
Couperie, Dom. de la 16
Cour de Blois, La 16

Coustille, Dom. de 140
Croix Belle, Dom. de la 68
Croix du Pin, La 84

Daubert, François 44
Daubert, François 44
Daumas Gassac, Mas de 72
Degenève, Laurent 140
Demeure-Pinet, Dom. 127
Destinea 29
Don Paolu, Dom. 112
Drôme 134
Duboeuf, Georges 85
Dyonysos 119

East France 135–41
Ellul-Ferrières, Dom. 85
Empeyron, Dom. d' 48
En Segur, Dom. d' 52
Errière, Dom. de l' 17
Esperance, Dom. d' 38

Fabre, Louis 86
Fadèze, Dom. de la 86
Faure, Dom. 87
Ferrandière, Dom. de la 87
Fleur des Landes 38
Flines, Dom. de 17
Fondacci, Dom. 123
Font-Mars, Dom. 88
Font Simian 120
Fontaine Aux Muses, Dom. la 141
Fontaine du Clos, Dom. 124
Fontenelles, Dom. de 55
Forton, Mas de 71
Four à Chaux, Dom. du 18
Frairie de la Moine, Dom. la 18
Franche-Comté 137–8

Garbelle, Dom. de 120
Gard 71–2
Gardrat, Dom. 35

Garonne 43–53
Gilles de Morban 53
Gillières, Dom. des 19
Goulotte, Dom. de la 140
Grand Ardèche 131
Grand Callamand, Dom. 124
Grand Cros, Le 116
Grand Fief, Dom. du 19
Grand Logis, Dom. du 20
Grange des Rouquette 88
Grollet, Dom. du 35

Hallopiere, Dom. de la 29
Haute-Marne 139
Hautes-Alpes 110–11
Hautes Noelles, Dom. les 20
Henriot, Pascal 138
Hérault 72–5
Higuère, Dom. de la 51
Hortala, J-M 66
Hospitaliers, Dom. des 56
Houssais, Dom. de la 21

Ile de Beauté 111–15
Ile Saint-Pierre, Dom. de l' 107
Imbardière, Dom. de l' 21
Instant Choisi 32
Intras, Mas d' 132

Janiny, Mas de 74
Jardin de la France 11, 13–29
Jarras, Dom. de 101
Jonquières, Dom, de 73
Jordy, Dom. 73
Joy, Dom. de 49

Laballe, Dom. de 41
Lafage, Dom. 65
Lamargue, Dom. 88
Landes 38
Languedoc-Roussillon 54–101
Lartigue, Dom. de 49
Laskar 125
Lauge, Dom. 89

Laure, Cellier de 118
Lauriers, Dom. des 89
Leyris Mazière 71
Loire Valley 11–29
Longue Tubi 117
Lot 53
Lot-et-Garonne 53
Lou Gaillot, Dom. 32
Lou Vin d'Aqui 105
Louanes, Dom. des 131

Madeleine, La 103
Mairan, Dom. de 90
Malavieille, Dom. de 90
Mallemort, Dom. de 91
Manoir de l'Hommelais 22
Mante, Mas de 60
Marie-Anaïs, Dom. de 67
Marotte, Dom. de 124
Marouine 117
Masques, Dom. des 109
Maurès 116–17
Meillan-Pages, Dom. 125
Meuse 139–41
Michelle, Dom. la 107
Mille et une Pierres 45
Minna Vineyard 108
Moderato 113
Moine Frères 36
Molines, Dom. de 72
Mont-Caume 118
Mont d'Hortes, Dom. de 69
Mont Saint-Jean, Dom. du 114
Montarels 69
Monte e Mare 113
Montel, Mas 91
Montels, Dom. de 46
Montfleury, Cave Cooperative de 132
Montlobre, Dom. de 92
Montplezy, Dom. 70
Monts de la Grage 75
Mosse, Dom. 58
Moulin, Dom. du 22
Moulin de la Touche, Le 23

...ines, Dom. de 74
...id Montsaugeonnais,
...e 139
Muzy, Dom. de 141

Negly, Ch. de la 66
Neuf Fiefs, Celliers des 92

Oc 76–100
Orviel, Dom. de l' 93

Pannier 23
Parc, Dom. du 24
Pastourette 117
Pays de la Garonne 43–53
Périgord 39
Perrière, La 24
Persenades, Dom. des 50
Pesquie, Chardonnay du 119
Petit Chateau, Dom. 25
Petit Chaumont, Dom. du 101
Petite Crau 118
Petrapiana, Dom. de 114
Pey-Neuf, Dom. du 118
Pierre-Belle, Dom. de 62
Pierre Blanche, Dom. de 25
Plan, Dom. le 134
Portes de Méditerranée 119
Preignes le Vieux, Dom. 93
Prestige du Condomois 46
Priés, Dom. des 26
Principauté d'Orange 119–20
Provence 102
Puits de Compostelle, Dom. du 12

Quatre Pilas, Dom. les 75
Quatre Routes, Dom. des 26

Ravanes, Dom. de 64
Régusse, Dom. de 103

Rey, Clos del 83
Rhône, Basse Vallée du 102
Ribonnet, Dom. de 44
Rieu Frais, Dom. du 133
Robineau, Michel 27
Rochanvigne, Dom. de 27
Rocherie, Dom. de la 28
Roque, Clos de la 60
Rosière, Dom. la 133
Rouge de Bachen 40
Rouillère, Cave de la 28
Rousset, Dom. de 104
Roustillan, Dom. de 134
Royal, Le 36

Sables du Golfe du Lion 101
St A. 37
Saint-Jean, Dom. de 104
Saint-Louis, Dom. de 94
Sainte Marthe, Dom. 56
Sainte-Marie-la-Blanche 141
Saint-Sardos 53
Saint-Vincent, Dom. 108
Saline, Dom. de 115
Salvat, Dom. 61
Sarrabelle, Dom. 51
Sautes, Dom. de 59
Sauvageonne, La 94
Skalli, Robert 95
Solstice 95
Sornin 37
Soulie, Dom. des 75
Suriane, Dom. de 109

Tain l'Hermitage, Cave de 129
Tariquet, Dom. du 50
Tarral 70
Tastet, Dom. du 41
Terra Mariana 115
Terra Sana 38
Terra Vecchia, Dom. 115
Terral, Cellier du 96
Terre Georges, Dom. 96
Terre Mégère, Dom. de 97

Terres Noires 97
Terroir du Var 105
Terroirs Landais 40–2
Thézac-Perricard 42
Thuerry 121
Tour Penedesses, Dom. de la 57
Tresbaudon, Dom. de 111
Triennes 120

Uby, Dom. d' 51

Valdaine, Cave de la 129
Valdition, Dom. de 108
Valvignères, Cave Cooperative de 133
Var 120–1
Vaucluse 121–5
Venesmes 12
Vermeil du Crès 98
Vernède, Dom. de la 98
Vernière, Dom. de la 13
Verriere Viognier, Dom. de la 125
Viaudière, Dom. de la 29
Vigne Blanche, Dom. 99
Vigne Lourac, Dom. 52
Vignerons Ardechois, Les 130
Vignes des Garbasses, Les 52
Vignoble de Flavigny 136
Vignoble Guillaume 137–8
Villaines-les-Prévôtes-Viserny 136
Villeneuve, Arnaud de 64
Vin de Domme 39
Vin de Fleur 45
Vin du Tsar 42
Viognier de la Galinière 106
Vivrant, Dom. 109

Winter Hill Reserve 99

Yeuses, Dom. les 100
Yonne 141